T0271936

# The Appropriation of Ecological Space

Although it is recognized that Thomas Robert Malthus was wrong when he posited a contradiction between population increase and agricultural growth, there are increasing signs that he could be proved right in the future. Perhaps Malthus was both too late and too early in his prediction.

He was too late, because he did not foresee the shift from land-based resources to fossil fuels, which did away with the limits of agricultural growth, at least temporarily; and he was too early to witness that fossil fuels would come up against their own limits in terms of supply as well as in terms of global warming.

This study deals with land-based resources and the role they play in the global socio-ecological metabolic regime, both today and in the future. In particular, the controversial use of agrofuels as a solution to coming scarcity is subjected to close scrutiny.

As a global society we are entering an era where land areas and land-based resources are coming to the fore once again for capital accumulation and economic growth after two centuries of fossil fuel dominance.

But land areas are limited, especially if we wish to curb deforestation to fight climate change. Then peak oil coexists with peak soil, and finding the land areas needed to supply food, feed, fibres and fuels to sustain a global population of nine, ten billion people will not be easily achieved.

On the contrary, this study maintains that economic power will translate into the appropriation of ecological space, land and land-based resources in various ways, through trade and environmental load displacements.

**Kenneth Hermele** is a Lecturer at the Universities of Lund and Gothenburg, Sweden. He received his PhD in Human Ecology from the University of Lund.

# Routledge studies in ecological economics

# The Appropriation of Ecological Space

Agrofuels, unequal exchange and environmental load displacements

**Kenneth Hermele**

 Routledge
Taylor & Francis Group

LONDON AND NEW YORK

First published 2014
by Routledge
2 Park Square, Milton Park, Abingdon, Oxon OX14 4RN

Simultaneously published in the USA and Canada
by Routledge
711 Third Avenue, New York, NY 10017

*Routledge is an imprint of the Taylor and Francis Group, an informa business*

© 2014 Kenneth Hermele

*British Library Cataloguing in Publication Data*
A catalogue record for this book is available from the British Library

*Library of Congress Cataloging in Publication Data*
A catalog record has been requested for this book

ISBN: 978-0-415-85834-2 (hbk)
ISBN: 978-0-203-79768-6 (ebk)

Typeset in Times New Roman
by Wearset Ltd, Boldon, Tyne and Wear

# Contents

# Illustrations

# Abbreviations

| | |
|---|---|
| APP | Área de Preservação Permanente [Area for Permanent Preservation] |
| BNDES | Banco Nacional do Desenvolvimento [Brazilian Development Bank] |
| BRIC | Brazil, Russia, India and China |
| CBD | common but differentiated responsibilities |
| CF | carbon footprint |
| CSO | civil society organization |
| DTA | domestic technology assumption |
| E | exa, quintillion, $10^{18}$ |
| ECLA | United Nations Economic Commission for Latin America |
| EF | ecological footprint |
| ELD | environmental load displacement |
| Embrapa | Empresa Brasileira de Pesquisa Agropecuária [Brazilian Agricultural Research Corporation] |
| EPA | Environmental Protection Agency |
| EROI | energy return on energy invested |
| EUE | ecologically unequal exchange |
| FAO | United Nations Food and Agriculture Organization |
| FDI | foreign direct investment |
| G | giga, billion, $10^9$ |
| GATT | General Agreement on Tariffs and Trade |
| GDP | gross domestic product |
| GFN | Global Footprint Network |
| GHG | greenhouse gases |
| glha | global hectares |
| ha | hectare |
| HANPP | human appropriation of net primary production |
| IEA | International Energy Agency |
| IPCC | Intergovernmental Panel on Climate Change |
| J | joule |
| kcal | kilocalorie |
| km | kilometre |

| | |
|---|---|
| LCA | life cycle analysis |
| M | million, $10^6$ |
| MA | Millennium Ecosystem Assessment |
| MFA | materials flow analysis |
| Mtoe | million tons of oil equivalents |
| NAC | new agricultural country |
| NGO | non-governmental organization |
| NIC | newly industrializing country |
| OECD | Organization for Economic Cooperation and Development |
| PPP | purchasing power parity |
| PSH | Prebisch–Singer hypothesis |
| PTB | physical trade balances |
| RED | Renewable Energy Directive |
| REDD+ | reduced emissions from deforestation and forest degradation |
| RL | Reserva Legal [Legal Reserve] |
| RSB | Roundtable on Sustainable Biofuels |
| t | ton |
| T | tera, trillion, $10^{12}$ |
| UN | United Nations |
| UNCTAD | United Nations Conference on Trade and Development |
| UNEP | United Nations Environment Programme |
| UNFCCC | United Nations Framework Convention on Climate Change |
| UNICA | União Nacional da Indústria de Cana-de-açúcar [Brazilian sugarcane industry association] |
| USDA | United States Department of Agriculture |
| W | watt |
| WEF | World Economic Forum |
| WF | water footprint |
| WTO | World Trade Organization |
| WWF | World Wildlife Fund |

# The argument

## The return of Malthus

It is a commonplace to say that Thomas Robert Malthus was wrong when over two hundred years ago he predicted an ever-wider gap between the need for food of a rapidly increasing population, and the restricted possibility of providing that food from a slowly growing rural economy. However, his thoughts are too often dismissed out of hand without pondering why he erred. Thinking about the "why" helps us understand that he was not so much wrong as too late *and* too early in his prediction.

Malthus was too late because he did not realize that the global socio-ecological metabolism – the dominant energy and resource flows of a society – was about to shift from renewable land-based sources to a regime based on fossil fuels, which did away with the limit to agricultural growth, at least temporarily; and he was too early to witness that fossil fuels would come up against their own limits in terms of supply as well as in terms of global warming. Put differently, Malthus was wrong when he posited an unresolvable contradiction between population increase and agricultural growth, but he may well be proven right in the future.

My hypothesis is that the last two hundred years – say from 1798 when Malthus anonymously published his *Essay on the Principle of Population*, until 1992 when the United Nations Framework Convention on Climate Change, UNFCCC, was launched – constitute an exception to the predominance of land-based resources, a respite created by reliance on fossil fuels. This way out of the Malthusian trap was complemented by the appropriation of ecological space – land areas – overseas, through trade and colonial occupation.

This exceptional period *could* be prolonged if we replace oil by coal or other fossil sources, such as "unconventional" oil and gas, but I will rule out this option on account of the negative climate impact such a turn would have. Likewise, I will disregard the appropriation of *more* forested land areas anywhere on the globe to produce agrofuels to replace fossil energy carriers, on the same ground: deforestation is one of the main drivers of climate change. As a consequence, we as a global society are limited to the land areas which already have been cleared for human use.

With these self-imposed limitations, peak oil co-exists with peak soil: today's five billion hectares of crop land and pastures have to suffice for the global socio-ecological metabolic needs of renewable resources for the production of food, feed, fibres and fuels.

However, to make do with these areas will not be easy, as a number of drivers are simultaneously increasing the demand for these very same areas: to meet economic, demographic, dietary and environmental needs will require more land areas. Against this background, one does not have to be Malthus to predict a conflict between the socio-ecological metabolic needs of a larger, wealthier and more meat-consuming global population, and the land areas available to produce the goods to satisfy these needs.

The global conflict over land and land-based resources is already playing itself out. Land areas are being "grabbed" in Africa, Asia, Latin America and Eastern Europe by an assortment of resource-hungry actors: pension and sovereign wealth funds, agro-businesses and energy conglomerates, states and local or international speculators, an appropriation of ecological space that is facilitated by international financial institutions.

Land grabbing is frequently a violent and conflictual process of "resolving" competing claims for land and land-based resources, violating the rights of the present holders and users of the land. This may be one explanation why land grabbing, as a particularly clear case of appropriation of ecological space, has gained a fair amount of attention recently. But two other forms of appropriation of ecological space have not: ecologically unequal exchange, and environmental load displacement, including trade in waste. I view these movements as essential vehicles for accessing land-based resources: importing ecological resources and disposing of waste – two land-based movements – underline the centrality of land areas to the global socio-ecological metabolic regime.

Agrofuels are illustrative of the conflicts concerning land areas and land-based resources which lie ahead of us. Agrofuels are promoted as energy-efficient, environmentally friendly, economically viable and geopolitically cautious, and they are held to be non-competitive with present land uses. But the opposite is true on every count: they are energy-doubtful, ecologically destructive, unviable without subsidies, and geopolitically risky, and they initiate a process of dramatic land-use change locally, nationally and globally, thus fanning global warming while further endangering biological diversity.

Of course, my argument is based on my two limiting assumptions: no fossil fuels, no deforestation. But even if we as a global system use coal or unconvential fossil sources to replace today's use of oil, the appropriation of ecological space will continue – although at a slower pace – and cause further deforestation. The various drivers looking for land areas are strong enough to keep up the pressure on the Earth's surfaces even without factoring in a substitution of agrofuels for fossil fuels. Just consider that as you have been reading this introductory argument, 247 forested hectares have been cleared somewhere around the globe (assuming that you have spent ten minutes by now: the global deforestation rate is approximately 13 million hectares annually; FAO 2005).

In what follows I will investigate the importance of land areas and land-based resources in three related aspects. Part I looks into the use of land in the global socio-ecological metabolic regime prior to the advent of fossil fuels, during the dominating reign of fossil energy, and into a hypothetical future of a re-emerging land-based socio-ecological metabolism. The focus is upon agrofuels, with a case study of Brazilian sugarcane ethanol.

Part II then turns to ecologically unequal exchange of land areas and land-based resources through various non-monetary metrics. If land has re-emerged as a strategic resource, as I argue, then gauging ecologically unequal exchange is one way to understand how power – purchasing power, economic power, military power – translates into appropriation of strategic space.

In Part III, I discuss the implications of this appropriation of ecological space and suggest that we are witnessing the emergence of a new agro-regime, where the fungibility of land and land-based resources – their substitutability, their multiple uses – explains their central role in providing ever more of food, feed, fibres and fuels.

Before I set out, a few basic data concerning global land use are given in Table I.1 for easy reference.

In what follows, I will use rounded figures – 1,500 million hectares of crop lands, 3,500 of pastures, and 5,000 of forests – in order to underline that my argument is based on simplifications regarding the trajectory – past, present, and future – of the global socio-ecological metabolic regime.

*Table I.1* Global land use, 2009–2010, million hectares

| | |
|---|---|
| Global land area | 13,003 |
| Crop lands | 1,534 |
| Pastures | 3,355 |
| Forests | 5,257 |

Source: FAO 2012, Tables 3 and 48.

# Part I

# Land use and agrofuels

Many demands are directed towards the limited land areas of the globe, and the possibility of meeting them all has been hotly debated. Do we, as a global society, live in a win–win world, or are we restrained by having to make stark choices, a situation best characterized by trade-offs? To be somewhat more specific: can the global desire for land to provide food, feed, fibres and fuels be met simultaneously; or will one kind of land use by necessity clash with, and rule out, other equally pressing needs?

No single kind of land use is more representative of the conflicting stances of "win-win" versus "trade-off" than the growing of feedstocks for agrofuels. This has nothing to do with the importance of agrofuels today – agrofuels are still quite insignificant in terms of both land use and energy volumes – but rather with the promise they hold out of being ecologically sustainable and climate neutral, a promise I will question in the following chapters.

To show the immensity of the task which we are confronting, I will start by returning to the metabolic shift which took place in the late 1700s and early 1800s from land-based energy sources to coal, and ask what a second transformation – now from fossil to renewable sources – would entail in terms of land-use change and conflicting demands on land.

From that vantage point I go on to look at today's most advanced producer of agrofuels, Brazil. We will see that agrofuels are being promoted by a coalition of energy and climate scientists, environmental non-governmental organizations, global corporations, international financial institutions, pension and sovereign wealth funds, and states in search of a win-win energy future.

These may sound like formidable opponents when even thinking about alternative future pathways for the socio-ecological metabolism, but I will show that accepting my two limiting assumptions does not preclude the possibility of imaging a future with many people living decent lives – if only we accept changing some of the basic assumptions of what such lifestyles entail. A future where the consumption of meat and the production of feedstocks for animals play a less dominating role than today would liberate huge swathes of land which could be used for agrofuels without entering into direct conflicts with the present use of the same lands.

# 1 The importance of land

For over two centuries, economics has been known as "the dismal science", a phrase which dates back to the nineteenth-century British historian Thomas Carlyle, who first applied it to Malthus (Levy and Peart 2001). Malthus, classical economist and priest, had earned this derogatory label by predicting a clash between population growth and agricultural production, as a result of "fixed laws of our nature". Though he later elaborated his argument further, it is his first simple formulation of 1798 which has remained in focus. Malthus wrote:

> I think I may fairly make two postulata.
>
> First, That food is necessary to the existence of man.
>
> Secondly, That the passion between the sexes is necessary, and will remain nearly in its present state.
>
> These two laws, ever since we have had any knowledge of mankind, appear to have been fixed laws of our nature; and, as we have not hitherto seen any alteration in them, we have no right to conclude that they will ever cease to be what they now are....
>
> Assuming, then, my postulata as granted, I say, that the power of population is indefinitely greater than the power in the earth to produce subsistence for man.
>
> Population, when unchecked, increases in a geometrical ratio. Subsistence increases only in an arithmetical ratio. A slight acquaintance with numbers will show the immensity of the first power in comparison of the second.
>
> (Malthus 2004/1798:12–13)

Why this disparity should exist between a geometric growth rate for population – 1, 2, 4, 8, 16, 32, 64 – and an arithmetic rate for agriculture – 1, 2, 3, 4, 5, 6, 7 – leading to population having grown nine times faster than agriculture after only six periods, Malthus never bothered to explain or substantiate. In a later edition of his work, he simply stated that his assertions were self-evident:

> The first of these propositions [population's geometrical growth] I considered as proved the moment the American [population] increase was

related, and the second proposition [agriculture's arithmetical growth] as soon as it was enunciated.

(Malthus 1801, quoted in Foster 2000:96)

This was not a wise stand to take, even then: instead of using the knowledge which existed regarding the factors conditioning population and agricultural growth rates, Malthus opted for pure conjecture. Based only on the example of the American rate of population increase – which he obtained from Benjamin Franklin – he devised a law of population growth which he then applied to England, a very different context; he further postulated that it would be valid forever, making the human propensity to procreate, in the colourful words of the environmental historian Donald Worster, equal to "a breeding machine" which goes on producing at the same steady rate, like "the new power loom" (Worster 1994:152).

## Two counter-arguments to Malthus

After publishing his essay, Malthus immediately reaped criticism for lacking an understanding of agriculture. In a surprisingly early formulation of the "metabolic rift", the Scottish economist James Anderson argued that the reason why agriculture did not improve in productivity was because it was deprived of what it needed in terms of manure and human waste. "Every person who has but heard of agriculture" he wrote in 1801, three years after Malthus,

> knows that animal manure, when applied to the soil, tends to add to its fertility; of course he must be sensible that every circumstance that tends to deprive the soil of that manure ought to be accounted an uneconomical waste highly deserving of blame.

(quoted in Foster 2000:145)

Thus, the limits to agriculture were not constituted by the available land areas, as Malthus thought, but originated from the failure to secure the re-application to agriculture of the resources which it had been bereaved of but which were essential in order to uphold its productivity. This is an argument which 66 years later was essential to Karl Marx's critique of agriculture during industrialization and early urbanization: the break in the circular flow of resources from countryside to town and back, blocking the development of agriculture. As Marx wrote in the first part of *Capital*:

> all progress in capitalist agriculture is a progress in the art, not only of robbing the worker, but of robbing the soil.... Capitalist production ... disturbs the metabolic interaction between man and the earth, i.e. it prevents the return to the soil of its constituent elements consumed by man in the form of food and clothing; hence it hinders the operation for the lasting fertility of the soil.

(Marx 1990/1867:637)

This, then, was one line of argument against the formula that Malthus had embraced: there was a man-made circumstance behind the slow productivity growth of agriculture, which, logically, could be removed if only man re-established the metabolic circular flow. To Marx, the need to import guano from Peru as fertilizer, bridging the rift, indicated that this metabolic break had stopped agriculture from being self-sustained (Foster 2000:156).

The dependence on guano also heralded a way of resolving the impasse of agriculture which since then has become the rule: instead of re-establishing a circular and renewable flow of resources, land areas and land-based resources were sourced overseas and imported into the centre of the global system.

One result of this appropriation of land-based resources was clear already after a couple of decades: the exploitation of guano, which had accumulated over thousands of years, was carried out at such a rapid pace that the resource base was destroyed. An island off the coast of Africa that had previously been covered with guano was soon "reduced to nothing but a plateau of bare rock", and even the guano islands outside Peru were, in the words of a contemporary observer, transformed into "vast sarcophagi" reminiscent of "death and the grave" (quoted in Clark and Foster 2012:76–77). Today, similar ruthless practices to access primary commodities continue under the label "mountain top removal", where whole mountains are blasted away.

There was also a second objection to Malthus's formula: the fact that he had neglected the contribution that scientific advancement could bring. Commenting on Malthus, Friedrich Engels wrote in 1844:

> Where has it been proved that the productivity of the land increases in an arithmetical progression? ... science increases at least as much as population. The latter increases in proportion to the size of the previous generation, science advances in proportion to the knowledge bequeathed to it by the previous generation, and thus under the most ordinary conditions also in a geometrical progression. And what is impossible to science?
>
> (Engels 1844)

Malthus's argument counter-posing arithmetic and geometric growth rates was so alluring that Engels applied the same imagery even as he criticized Malthus: according to Engels not only population but also agriculture would increase geometrically.

## Boserup: no laws of agriculture

A hundred and twenty-one years later, in the early 1960s, economist Ester Boserup argued that agricultural development was a much more dynamic story than the straitjacket Malthus had assumed, and that population pressure could be a driver for higher agricultural productivity, thus removing the conflict that he had stipulated. She thought that the impact of population growth often was a positive one, and that "the population within a given land area can double several times without having to face either starvation or lack of employment opportunities in agriculture" (Boserup 1965:117). However, Boserup's standpoint had more to do with a belief in the capacity of peasants to gradually adapt to changing circumstances than with Engels's trust in the advance of science. Still, her reasoning is frequently reduced to a one-dimensional counter-argument to Malthus's equally simplified thesis, as the above quotation may lead you to conclude: against his strict contradiction of population versus agriculture, Boserup is held to believe that a growing population is the mother of invention.

But in fact Boserup argued that population growth *may* result in an intensification of the use of land, not that it always would. Increasing population pressure on limited land areas, Boserup thought, might drive peasants to develop area-intensive methods in order to maximize the crop yield per hectare.

Thus, according to Boserup contrary to Malthus, there were no "laws" at play but only contingent relationships, where the outcome could be either positive or negative. As Boserup sums up on one of the first pages of her study:

> It is not to be denied that the food potential of the world has been narrowed down by populations, who did not know how to match their growing numbers by more intensive land use without spoiling the land for a time or forever. But nevertheless, the neo-Malthusian theories … are misleading, because they tend to neglect the evidence we have of growing populations which managed to change their methods of production in such a way as to preserve and improve the fertility of their land…. Growing populations may in the past have destroyed more land than they improved, but it makes little sense to project past trends into the future, since we know more and more about methods of land preservation and are able, by means of modern methods, to reclaim much land, which our ancestors have made sterile.
>
> (Boserup 1965:22)

This is a surprisingly open position at the outset of Boserup's study, and one which she is not remembered for having held. Here, Boserup actually goes along with Malthus's tenet of a contradiction between population and agriculture by conceding that a growing population may destroy the land upon which it lives, only to conclude that "we" in the future need not repeat such mistakes.

## Malthus: no limits to growth

Malthus and Boserup have remained the opposing poles in the population–agriculture discourse, and anyone entering the debate customarily refers to both of them, usually decrying Malthus and celebrating Boserup. But although Malthus, as we have seen, was severely criticized and even ridiculed for his position as soon as his essay was published, nothing seems to have stopped the advance of the Malthusian formula in the public consciousness: Worster claims that Malthus's "ironclad ratios and his warnings of impending national apocalypse" have become "part of the folklore of capitalism" (Worster 1994:152–153). It may well have been, as the economic historian Eric Roll assumes, the fact that Malthus expressed his argument in such a simple formula that explains why his theory was seen as "spectacular", leading to both "support and criticism in abundance" (Roll 1961:196).

Malthus has been identified with one of the crucial issues of economic and social development, the question of limits to growth, and Worster maintains that Malthus "introduced a new ecological dimension to Adam Smith's study of human economics" (Worster 1994:150). But Malthus himself felt the need to attenuate his original unwavering position, and in later editions of his essay he softened some of his positions in a final chapter called "Of our Rational Expectations respecting the Future Improvement of Society":

> On the whole ... though our future prospects respecting the mitigation of the evils arising from the principle of population may not be so bright as we could wish, yet they are far from being entirely disheartening, and by no means preclude ... gradual and progressive improvement in human society.
> (quoted after the 1809 American edition, Volume II, Chapter 12:499)

And he had already asserted in the first edition of his essay: "No limits whatever are placed to the productions of the earth; they may increase for ever and be greater than any assignable quantity" (Malthus 2004/1798:18). Nevertheless, and although his lack of ecological concerns has been noticed (see Foster 2000:92–93, and Martínez-Alier 1990:10), Malthus has come to be seen as the symbol of a whole dismal tradition which forecasts the end of growth and even development. Today, should one venture to question that economic growth can go on eternally and resource use expand forever, one should expect to be branded a "neo-Malthusian".

However, recognizing that Malthus made an important point in turning our attention to the possibility of a conflict between a society's metabolic needs and available land areas to meet those needs should not refrain us from criticizing the mistake he committed when he presented his theory, in the words of economic historian Richard Wilkinson, "as a law valid for all time" (Wilkinson 1973:22–23). He did not realize that he was standing exactly at the turning point when Britain was about to initiate a transition from one metabolic regime to another, from solar and land-based to fossil energy, thus temporarily doing away with, in the words of historian Rolf Peter Sieferle, "the first and the most important characteristic of the agrarian solar energy system", its "dependency upon territory" (Sieferle 2001:25).

Therefore, instead of giving a credible forecast for the future development path of societies, Malthus summed up what *had been* the limiting conditions, which would not constitute a restraint on economic growth thenceforth, at least not until today's double peak of oil and soil. As economist Paul Krugman correctly observes, Malthus "was right about roughly 58 out of 60 centuries of civilization.... We only think Malthus got it wrong because the two centuries he was wrong about were the two centuries that followed the publication of his work" (Krugman 2009).

## Ecological windfalls from coal and colonial occupation

At the time of Malthus's writing, the basic limiting production factor in Britain was not capital, nor labour, but rather land; hence, what ushered Britain into an industrial mode of production and a new socio-ecological metabolic regime was that it managed to break the constraints imposed on growth and development by its scarce resource, land.

Britain's land limits were shifted in time and space, from agricultural lands to coal, and from Britain to its colonies. In this way, Britain appropriated land areas below its own ground as well as above ground across the sea. As summarized by historian Kenneth Pomeranz:

> the significance of the Atlantic trade [resides] not in terms of financial profits and capital accumulation, nor in terms of demand for manufactures – which Europe could have probably generated enough of at home – but in terms of how much they relieved the strain on Europe's supply of what was truly scarce: land and energy.
>
> (Pomeranz 2000:23)

Taken together with the use of its own coal, the cross-Atlantic trade gave Britain a windfall gain which led it "*out* of a world of Malthusian constraints" (Pomeranz 2000:23), or, as we might rephrase it, out of the dismal world forecasted by Malthus, thus liberating capital accumulation in Britain from the limits imposed by land.

Already in Britain's exchange with the United States of America, its former colony, we find a case of unequal exchange: the US was sending more and receiving less in terms of embodied labour and land, and Britain was receiving more and sending less. ("Embodied" labour and land refer to the labour and land used to bring forth a product, not its actual content. In the jargon of the environmental movement, such embodiment is often called a product's "rucksack".) Comparing the flows around 1850 of embodied labour hours and land areas in one thousand pounds sterling of US cotton cloth and one thousand pounds sterling of British textiles, the raw cotton imported by Britain embodied eight times as many labour hours and 60 times as much land as British textiles sold for the same amount (Hornborg 2007a:267–268). With the terminology I use here, Britain appropriated ecological space (and labour) from the US via trade.

## The significance of the shift to a mineral regime

Demographer E.A. Wrigley has observed that Britain in the eighteenth century was being transformed from an organic to a mineral economy. He notes that in an organic economy, most resource use is tied to "the fixed supply of land and … its organic products" (Wrigley 1988:5), and then goes on to list the land-based products central to the old regime: food, feed, fibres, leather, textiles and construction materials. In other words, an organic economy is almost totally dependent on, and restricted by, land areas.

In a mineral economy, on the other hand, the land limitation is suspended, temporarily, as the key economic activities increasingly come to use energy in the form of mineral resources to replace draught animals and human power:

> Always previously a productive agriculture had been the base of the whole span of economic activity because all industrial processes depended principally or exclusively on organic raw materials. The new [mineral] age was built upon different foundations. The fruits of the earth were increasingly used as food alone. It was not from the soil but from beneath the soil that the raw materials of a new economic age were drawn.
>
> (Wrigley 1988:73)

Wrigley recounts a telling example: in 1840, by its use of steam power, France benefited from the equivalent of one million workers (in horse power). The steam engines can thus be said to be, to use the image applied by contemporary economist and statistician Pierre Émile Levasseur, "true slaves, the most sober, docile and tireless that could be imagined". By 1887, the steam power capacity of France equalled 98 million people, "deux esclaves et demi par habitant de la France" (two-and-a-half slaves for every Frenchman; quoted in Wrigley 1988:76). Wrigley points out that "Englishmen, of course, were slave owners on a much larger scale", as the British steam engine capacity was more than twice that of France (ibid.).

The need to be area-efficient – the concern of Boserup – in order to avoid competition between energy and food was an argument mobilized to support large-scale investments in transport infrastructure that were debated in Britain at this juncture. Since each horse needed four to eight acres of hay annually, canals and railroads would free up large tracts of land to grow food for human consumption by replacing horses with barges and trains which relied on coal. As an engineer reflecting upon a proposed canal about 1800 concluded: "How desirable any improvement that will lessen the keep of horses" (quoted in Wilkinson 1973:123–124). In 1833, a report to the House of Commons on "steam carriages" presented quite a straightforward argument:

> It has been said that in Great Britain there are above a million of horses engaged in various ways in the transport of passengers and goods, and that to support each horse requires as much land as would upon an average support eight men. If this quantity of animal power were displaced by steam-engines, and the means of transport drawn from the bowels of the earth, instead of being raised upon its surface, then, supposing the above calculation correct, as much land would become available for the support of human beings as would suffice for an additional population of eight millions.
>
> (quoted in Wilkinson 1973:124–125)

The surface of the Earth was obviously the scarce resource to protect here, and "the bowels" – coal – provided the solution to competing land uses.

The limits of the land-based metabolic regime can also be illustrated by posing a counter-factual question: could the transformation from agriculture to industry which occurred in Britain have taken place without the transition to land-saving fossil energies? Well, only with great difficulty, as four Britains would have been needed by World War I to produce just the required volumes of charcoal for the iron-ore smelters in the absence of coal, not to mention other uses of charcoal (Sieferle 2001:122). And had Britain not had fossil coal available, it would have needed five times its entire merchant fleet *all year round* to transport the forest produce necessary to replace its actual coal consumption of 1790 (Sieferle 2001:107–108). Likewise, a hypothetical exercise shows that Britain would have needed its whole land area by 1850, and five times that by 1900, just to be able to substitute its use of fossil fuels by hypothetical forest biomass (Schandl and Krausmann 2007:120–121). And similarly for agricultural products which were imported from the colonies to Britain. Just to substitute wool for the cotton which was brought to Britain in 1815 would have required grazing sheep on areas larger than the combined crop and pasture lands of Britain (Pomeranz 2000:276).

Britain's coal deposits also helped to fuel other countries, such as Denmark, which made use of British coal to replace the energy it previously had obtained from its now disappearing forests. In the 1760s, almost every ship which called on Copenhagen from Britain carried coal (Kjærgaard 1994:120). Thinking counter-factually about what would have happened had this ecological relief not come about, historian Thorkild Kjærgaard paints a gloomy picture indeed, for Denmark as well as for Europe as a whole: "an entropic nightmare" where people

> might have wandered about, shivering with cold and searching for dried cowpats to provide a little heat and with which to cook, and there might not have been enough wood to make as much as a handle. Ecological chaos would have reigned, marked by hitherto unknown degrees of sand drift [common in Denmark at the time], increasingly violent hydrological disturbances, and unmercifully decreasing agricultural production.
>
> (Kjærgaard 1994:125)

The limits that a solar, land-based regime set for development and growth were thus removed by a fossil-fuelled growth path which for two centuries, combined with scientific advancement of the kind envisioned by Engels, and by the ecological relief that imports of land-based resources from the empires achieved, invalidated Malthus's forecast. In fact, the limits were not dissolved but only displaced in time and space; in due course they would re-emerge. But in the meantime, the metabolic needs of Europe were shifted not only elsewhere, to colonial lands, but also "elsewhen", to use sociologist William Catton's innovative word, to fossil fuels (Catton 1980:41).

Two hundred years ago, transport capacity was far from sufficient for the enormous volumes of traded goods that the metabolic shift required, but soon new vessels, new ports, and new routes jointly enabled the import of ever-increasing volumes of appropriated ecological space. This is the real significance of the construction of the Suez and Panama canals, ready for use in 1869 and 1914 respectively: they were made necessary by the speedy transition to a new metabolic regime. At the same time, in a recursive process, they facilitated and helped speed up the arrival of this new regime.

The benefits of this revolution in transport and energy in terms of greater access to crucial resources were immediate for the colonial power: India's exports to Britain of grain increased threefold between 1875 and 1900 (from three to ten million tons), and amounted by the end of the nineteenth century to as much as one-fifth of Britain's total wheat consumption (Davis 2002:299).

Just as the transitions in Britain from land surfaces to minerals, and from local to overseas resources, were accompanied and facilitated by a greatly increased transport capacity, the exploitation of hinterlands by cities was speeded up when railways replaced horses to become the main transporter of raw materials to the urban factories, and then again for distributing the produce back out of the cities.

Historian William Cronon shows this relationship for Chicago, a city which drew its life blood from a vast hinterland, criss-crossed by railways, roads and waterways, to secure its needs of raw materials, timber and cattle from the countryside. As a resident of Chicago concluded in 1893: "Without farmers there could be no cities" (quoted in Cronon 1991: 97). The logic can also be turned around: without cities, the countryside would look very different. This is perhaps not a sensational insight, but nevertheless something which is frequently overlooked. As Cronon stresses when he summarizes the relationship between Chicago and its supply areas: disregarding the relationship with the hinterland obscures the real implication of the exchange which takes place. The urban landscape with its streets, stores and people is premised on a gigantic but "absent" – that is, invisible – countryside. What look like urban "temples of commerce" are in fact dependent on "mausoleums of landscapes vanishing from the city's hinterland", as Cronon graphically states (Cronon 1991:263).

A famous advertisement from the early 1900s shows this clearly, and somewhat ironically. The leading Chicago department store Montgomery Ward, the tallest building in Chicago at the time, markets itself as a "busy bee-hive", alluding to nature and industrious insects which bring goods to the city's population. But the only production premises shown in the ad are factories, without relationship to agriculture or to any hinterland. The Montgomery Ward "bee-hive" is self-sustained, or so it would seem.

But this is only one side of the coin. Montgomery Ward was not just a huge department store; it also sold its goods via mail order catalogues throughout the country, thus reaching out to the hinterland that its advertisements neglected. Cronon visualizes "millions of families around the country with dog-eared [Montgomery] Ward and [the competing] Sears catalogues sitting at their kitchen tables [holding] innumerable dinner table conversations about possible purchases" and concludes that we stand in front of "a landscape of obscured connections": "The ecological place of production grew ever more remote from the economic point of consumption, making it harder and harder to keep track of the true costs and consequences of any particular product" (Cronon 1991:340).

It was not only the origin of the inputs which was hidden; the disposal of waste also remained obscured, and the full extent of the flows which preconditioned the existence of cities were hidden from view. The nature of the situation is well captured by the case of Hong Kong (Newcombe *et al.* 1978). A small land area with high population density and an impressive industrial capacity, Hong Kong, even before becoming part of China, drew on land areas and water-based resources of the Chinese mainland and the ocean waters surrounding it, sourcing its needs and depositing its waste outside of its borders, including in the global commons (the sea and the atmosphere). In this way, Hong Kong "occupies" 220 times its own surface in order to secure the renewable resources it consumes in one year; if we add the hypothetical land area needed to absorb the carbon dioxide emissions of Hong Kong, then its total "ecological footprint" is more than 300 times larger than its land area (Boyden *et al.* 1981:115–119, and Warren-Rhodes and Koenig 2001:349).

## Concluding remarks

The perspective of the metabolism of cities, such as Hong Kong, and of individual companies, such as Montgomery Ward, can also be applied to countries. Looking at societies as socio-metabolic regimes has, at least since the days of Karl Marx, been a fruitful way to understand the relationship economy-nature: agrarian and industrial economies show systematic differences between what may be termed a land-based agrarian and a fossil-based industrial regime. The differences are consequential, as can be seen from Table 1.1.

While the industrial metabolic regime uses 3–12 times as much material per capita as the agricultural regime, and 7–30 times as much energy per hectare,

*Table 1.1* Socio-ecological metabolic regimes compared

|  | Agrarian | Industrial | Difference as ratio of industrial to agrarian |
| --- | --- | --- | --- |
| Population density, capita/km² | <40 | 100–300 | 2.5–7.5 |
| Material use, tons/capita/year | 2–5 | 15–25 | 3–12 |
| Energy use, GJ/ha/year | 20–30 | 200–600 | 7–30 |
| Biomass energy share, % | 95–100 | 10–30 | 0.1–0.3 |
| Fossil fuel energy share, % | 0–5 | 60–80 | 12–80 |
| Material use, tons/ha/year | 1–2 | 20–50 | 10–50 |

Sources: Fischer-Kowalski *et al.* 2007, Table 8.1, and Krausmann *et al.* 2008, Table 1.

Note
GJ=gigajoule=billion joules.

and while its fossil energy share is 12–80 times as large, its dependency on biomass energy is 3–10 times *less* than in the average agrarian regime.

The explanation for these differences, as I have argued, is that fossil fuels were substituted for land-based resources, thus avoiding the problem that limited land restricted further capital accumulation and economic growth. This new industrial regime has by now spread also to regions of the global system which until recently were dominated by the land-based agrarian mode. The impact in terms of global flows is staggering: see Figure 1.1.

All in all, the global material flows – construction minerals, ores, fossil fuels and biomass – have multiplied sevenfold in a little over a hundred years, from less than ten billion tons in 1900 to close to 70 billion tons today. In absolute terms, biomass use also multiplied, although it has lost the dominant position it occupied in 1900.

My assumption regarding the twin peaks of oil and soil implies that land areas and land-based resources are re-emerging as essential strategic resources, thus becoming of concern to the wielders of political, economic and military power, be they countries, national and international institutions, or corporations. This means that we are entering a new phase where the absent aspect (to use Cronon's term) of the metabolism of economies is giving way to a situation where ever

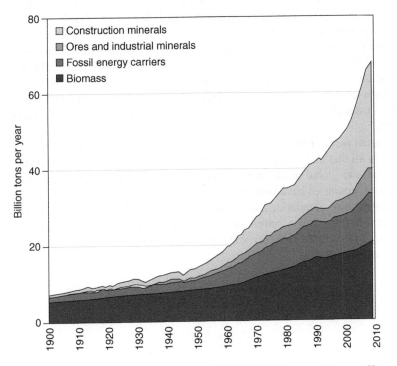

*Figure 1.1* Global materials extraction, 1900–2009, billion tons (source: Krausmann *et al.* 2009; used with permission).

more open attention will be dedicated to land areas, land-based resources, and raw materials in general. As Alexander Haig testified as early as 1980 to the US Congress (at this time Haig had left his position as chief commander of NATO forces but had not yet been appointed Secretary of State by President Reagan): "the era of 'resource wars' has arrived" (quoted in Klare 2002:236). In this perspective, growing conflicts over land areas and land-based resources are to be expected.

To resource analyst Michael Klare, Haig's welcoming of the opportunity to go to war to secure the flow of material resources is reminiscent of previous US imperial strategies. The difference, says Klare, is that the resources which are considered strategic today include water and timber, in addition to oil (Klare 2002:7). With my postulated twin peaks – peak oil, peak soil – I would add agricultural land in general to the list of strategic resources, the land areas needed to produce food, feed, fibres and fuels. After all, soldiers are also dependent on land areas for their metabolic needs.

There exists a terrifying historic parallel here: the dependency upon land areas and land-based resources has in the past opened the door to some of the most dreadful experiences of hunger and starvation in the history of mankind. In the late nineteenth century, large-scale famine was caused by the subordination of local needs to the metabolic requirements of the imperial power, Great Britain. The outcome was a death toll estimated at 30–60 million people in famines in India, China and Brazil, 1876–1879 and 1896–1900 (Davis 2002:7). The Earth's population around 1900, was 1.7 billion people; today, with a global population of seven billion, the proportional number of victims would amount to as many as 126–241 million people. At the same time, however, exports of grain from India continued to Britain, as we have seen; had this appropriation of ecological space by Britain in the midst of frightful mass starvation not taken place, it has been estimated, 25 million people in India could have been saved (Davis 2002:310).

The present race for land areas and land-based resources presents a situation which is not all that dissimilar: a growing appropriation of land by various local, international and global actors at the same time that many poor, but resource- and land-rich, countries have been robbed of state capacity and have no reserves to protect their own populations, had they been so inclined. They are suffering a dismal harvest following a couple of decades of neo-liberal policies after the debt crisis of the 1980s, with privatization and commoditization of land areas and land-based resources.

# 2 Land-use scenarios for agrofuels and nine billion people

Forecasting an increase in the importance of land-based resources has become more common as we have witnessed a new pattern of price movements for raw materials in general and food in particular during the last decade. This started four years into the twenty-first century, when food and primary commodity prices began to rise almost vertically, and it appeared at first to culminate in 2008, when they hit their highest level since the oil price hikes of the mid-1970s, still the pinnacle in post-war raw materials prices. For instance, the raw materials price index reached approximately 225 in 2008, but although it had more than doubled in just a few years this was still not enough to match the level of the mid-1970s of approximately 340 (UNCTAD 2011, index 2000 = 100).

Following the financial crisis of 2008, prices plummeted as expected, but a year later they began climbing again, reaching and then surpassing the 2008 pre-crisis record level as early as 2011. This was surprising: for almost 50 years, food prices had been low and stable, with the 1970s a brief exception to the general downwards-sloping trend. Now, however, a reverse trend appears to be establishing itself: see Figure 2.1.

These are short-term price movements, of course, and not essential to my argument, which is long-term and structural; but I believe they herald a new phase of dependency on land areas and land-based resources.

## Drivers behind the new price trend

The causes for the price movements of the early twenty-first century are contentious, and no consensus as to the respective importance of the various drivers has been reached. One issue has been what importance to attribute to the growth of land areas dedicated to agrofuels in Brazil (sugarcane ethanol), the USA (maize ethanol), and the EU (rape seed biodiesel), just to mention the largest producers, as agrofuels compete with food for humans, directly (grains) or indirectly (soy and maize for animal feed). In the US, the share of the maize harvest used for ethanol was 30 per cent, while the share of rape seed going to biodiesel in the EU was as high as 60 per cent (von Braun 2008). These are important land areas, certainly, but *how* important is not easy to say, as many equally influential factors were at play.

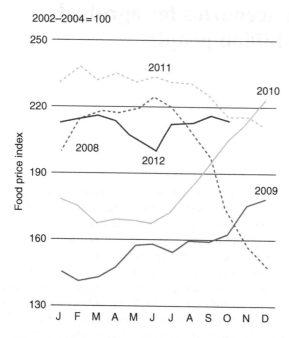

*Figure 2.1* FAO Food Price Index, 2008 – October 2012 (source: FAO 2012a; used with permission).

In addition to the increased use of land for agrofuels, droughts were recorded in major producing countries such as Australia; simultaneously, oil prices rose steeply and reached US$140 a barrel in 2008, all of which prompted a growing number of speculative contracts for food and feedstocks, which pushed prices still higher. Add to this the increasing demand for food and meat from a wealthier and more numerous world population, and anything but increasing prices would have been surprising.

Perhaps the combination of low stocks and speculation in food and other land-based resources was particularly problematic. The global stocks of the main cereals – rice, wheat, and maize – had been going down: in 2001/2002 they stood at close to 600 million tons; by 2003/2004, they had fallen to a little over 400 million tons, and this dangerously low level was maintained in 2006/2007 and 2007/2008 (FAO 2012c).

Added to this was a surge of speculation in agricultural and other primary commodities, which can be traced back to the early 1990s when Goldman Sachs, as the first of the major global bankers, started selling a new "product", the Goldman Sachs Commodity Index Fund. As other banks and finance institutions followed suit, the "business segment" exploded from US$13 billion in 2003 to US$317 billion in 2008, a 24-fold increase in just five years. Then the crash came, and the forecasted growth of this "instrument" into the trillion-dollar bracket had to be postponed (Kaufman 2010:27, 32).

Given this complexity, allocating shares to the respective drivers is better left undone, but the literature is nevertheless awash with statements targeting one or the other, selecting one as the main cause for the price rises, with a special penchant for the role of agrofuels, the newest addition to the demand-pushers. At one extreme, agrofuel production is seen as the main culprit behind the price increase, much more important than any of the others. According to an influential World Bank report, the impact of higher energy prices (on fertilizer prices and transport costs) is responsible for only 25–30 per cent of the total food price increase, while "most of the remaining 70–75 per cent increase in food commodities prices was due to agrofuels" (Mitchell 2008:17). Other factors, for instance the export bans which were imposed by some exporting countries in order to prevent food riots and improve the local availability of food, were seen as secondary consequences caused by the growth of agrofuels.

At the opposite end of the spectrum, the agrofuel lobby plays down the role of agrofuels, calling it "only one among a myriad of factors that drove up commodity prices" (Garten Rothkopf 2009:498). Although this perspective, like the previous one, takes note of the plethora of contributing causes, their relative weights are inverted: agrofuels are now seen to be insignificant. In a similar vein, Monsanto, a major agribusiness corporation, maintained that "grain shifting to the production of biofuels represents only a small part of increased food prices", while the major responsibility rests with the rising cost of oil. In a web-comment, Monsanto concluded: "there is virtually no connection to biofuels and these unfortunate shortages around the globe" (Monsanto 2009).

The International Food Policy Research Institute opted for adducing a responsibility of 30 per cent of the food price rise to agrofuels, mostly on account of the toll that ethanol took on the supply of maize in the USA (von Braun 2008:5). This relative weight for agrofuels has now become standard. For instance, the Food and Agriculture Organization of the United Nations (FAO), after reviewing the literature, concludes that there is no consensus about the impact of agrofuels but nevertheless maintains that they have contributed 30–40 per cent to the upswing for internationally traded maize, and "somewhat less" for other basic commodities (FAO 2009a:5).

There are in fact so many factors involved here that attributing the relative share to the various drivers for the rise in food prices is not possible with a reasonable degree of certainty. Several studies testify to this and simply conclude that the picture is complex and that it is best not to be too definite about the respective impact of each driver. In other words, no-one really knows. Still, a recent analysis of the price hike concludes, as confidently as all the others, that speculation "played a key role", while it found "no evidence" for a link with stronger demand from China and India, and only "some role" for agrofuels (Baffes and Haniotis 2010:18).

China's role in the price trend has been misunderstood. It is true that China was not overly *dependent* on the imports of cereals prior to the 2008 price rises;

in fact China was a net exporter of cereals during the three years leading up to the price spike, 2005/2006–2007/2008. China nevertheless had become one of the major *importers* of agricultural products (not just food) toward the end of the decade (FAO 2009b:18–19). At the same time, US surpluses sold on the global market decreased significantly (WTO 2009 and 2011, Table II:15). Thus, although China probably did not create the price rise of 2004–2008, it may have been responsible for keeping prices up.

I believe that these two trends taken together – an increase in demand from China and a diminution in supply from the US – will be the main drivers for the future. This is also the conclusion that the FAO has more recently come around to, after some wavering. In 2009 the FAO held that China (and India) had nothing to do with the price rises of food and agricultural products of the pre-crisis years, but it has subsequently changed its verdict and now concludes that two trends jointly share the responsibility: the increase in imports to Asia, and the levelling off of exports from North America as of 2007 (FAO 2009b:19 and FAO 2011:75, respectively).

## The double fungibility of land

My central concern, however, is not to allocate percentages to the various factors pushing prices upwards, but to consider the inter-connectedness of markets and of land uses. The reason is that there exists a large degree of substitutability among feedstocks for similar or competing purposes: maize and soybean are used for human consumption, as animal feed, and as feedstocks for fuels (ethanol and biodiesel, respectively); sugarcane is used as sweetener as well as for ethanol; rape seed and palm oil are used for biodiesel and as inputs to the food industry. This reinforces the point I made in my introductory argument about the fungibility of land: not only is land fungible, but agricultural feedstocks have substitutable uses. In effect, land is doubly fungible.

Consider the impact of using US maize to produce ethanol for the US market: as maize is diverted from animal feed to produce ethanol, American hogs must be fed by other products, for instance by importing maize from Argentina, the second largest exporter after the US. And when soybean production in Argentina is turned over to produce biodiesel, the global food industry may be stimulated to look for substitutes from palm oil plantations in Indonesia and Malaysia – and vice versa, if biodiesel plants use Asian palm oil as feedstock. Or when Brazil enlarges the land areas planted with sugarcane and soybean, Brazilian cattle ranchers may be pushed onto new lands, inside and outside of Brazil. Put another way, what may appear to be independent land-use changes are in fact a series of linked events, one market impacting the others.

The fungibility of land and its produce makes it reasonable to pit agrofuels against food, for instance by arguing that we feed cars instead of people: the areas around the world dedicated to producing the ethanol and biodiesel used in the European Union in 2008 could instead have been used to support 127 million people for a whole year (Oxfam 2012). The fungibility of land and the feedstocks used to produce agrofuels makes such comparisons more than just a moral stance; they indicate a real contradiction, given the fact that the available land areas are limited.

Allotting responsibility for price movements to individual drivers in this situation runs the risk of missing the inter-dependencies: a movement in one market may cause significant knock-on effects in various other markets. Focusing on which of the many factors is the most important force in pushing up the prices of food and primary commodities may hide the real issue: the centrality of land-based resources to the global socio-ecological metabolism today, and still more in the future.

## Agrofuels and land-use scenarios: how much is possible?

The focus on agrofuel as driver of food price movements should be seen against the background of the recent surge of studies set out to assess their potential to replace fossil fuels. The point of departure for such studies is not that biomass and agrofuels today play an important role in the global energy system; they do not. Biomass as a whole accounts for 10 per cent of global energy use, and out of this only 2 per cent is used as liquid fuel for transport (see Figures 2.2 and 2.3). Why dedicate so much attention to something which is 2 per cent of 10 per cent, i.e. two per thousand, of global energy use? The answer has much to do with geopolitics and energy security.

The present phase of agrofuel expansion began in Brazil in the mid-1970s, when the military government initiated the Pro-Álcool – pro-alcohol – programme in order to increase its energy independence and reduce import costs in the aftermath of the oil price increases in 1973–1974. Similarly, in 2005 the US Congress mandated in its Energy Independence and Security Act that 137 billion litres of agrofuels be sold on the US market by 2022, twice the global production of ethanol. More recently, the EU has mandated a doubling of renewables in its

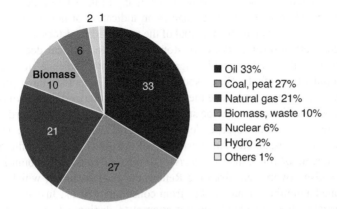

*Figure 2.2* World energy supply, 2009, percentages (source: based on IEA 2011a:6).

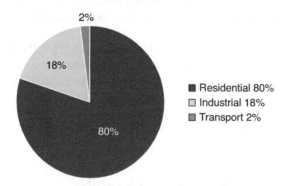

*Figure 2.3* Global use of biomass for energy, *c*.2000, percentages (source: based on FAO 2008:11).

fuel mix by 2020. Hence, geopolitics is at the core of today's craving for agro-fuels, a situation which the arrival of peak oil cannot help but reinforce.

Against this background, it makes sense that many studies to estimate the global agrofuel potential have appeared recently. But these assessments, based as they are on wildly different assumptions, arrive at wildly diverging outcomes. For instance, which feedstocks should be the mainstay of agrofuel production in the scenario? The choice will decide the result in terms of reduced dependency on fossil fuels, greenhouse gas balance, production volumes, and geographic location of agricultural lands, as well as possible conflicts with other land uses.

Enter the review article, where a number of individual studies are summed up, more often than not leading to the conclusion that the "truth" is somewhere in the middle range of the reviewed studies. (See for instance Berndes *et al.* 2003, who cover 17 studies of the potential contribution of biomass to global energy supply, and Haberl *et al.* 2010, summarizing ten studies). The average values thus have a tendency to be classified as reasonable, while in fact many of the studies are unrealistic and not to be taken seriously, other than as an indication of how eager the pro-agrofuel interests are to inflate the potential of the promoted feedstocks.

The analytical merry-go-round does not stop here. When political decisions are imminent, there is the need to decide once and for all what "science" tells us about the potential of agrofuels. Since social and natural scientists have presented different guesstimates, and since they have then summarized their own or their colleagues' studies in terms of wide spans of probabilities, the final word to guide decision-makers goes to "independent" consultants who do not have any axes to grind (or so it is assumed). An illustration of this practice is the influential *Gallagher Review of the Indirect Effects of Biofuels Production*, commissioned by the British government from the Renewable Fuels Agency, which in turn commissioned a number of sub-studies from consultancy firms. Just as in so many review articles, the consultants do not attempt to distinguish good from bad estimates, and the wide spans are replicated (*Gallagher Review* 2008).

As time presses on, finally, international organizations such as the FAO, the United Nations Environment Programme (UNEP), the World Bank, and the Intergovernmental Panel on Climate Change (IPCC), feel the need to rule on which feedstocks are the best, how greenhouse gas emissions are to be computed, and whether direct or indirect land-use change should be included. This is intended to lay the ground for global politics and for agreeing on certification standards.

At the same time, and feeding this flood of studies, reviews, assessments and summaries, natural scientists are eagerly devising new, better, more efficient feedstocks and processes. From first-generation ethanol, based on sugarcane and maize, there is increasing talk of second-generation (based on cellulose, opening up the prospect of using fast-growing species, grasses and forestry residues) and even third-generation agrofuels (based on algae), all of which, of course, will lead to further studies.

## Three approaches to the study of future land use

Towards the end of the 1990s, a number of worrying studies were presented which echoed the re-emergence of the Malthusian perspective on the significance of limits on land-based resources. The reports highlighted the difficulty of producing enough food for a growing world population which was also becoming wealthier, leading to a diet of more animal products and more calories (Brown and Kane 1995; Daily *et al.* 1998; Dyson 1999; Pinstrup-Andersen *et al.* 1999).

What is striking when one reads these accounts today is that they totally failed to foresee the role that agrofuels would play in the scenario constructions which have appeared since, the first ones just a few years later. While these late twentieth-century scenarios do account for food-supply bottlenecks related to decreasing agricultural yields, and while they do factor in growing populations and new consumption and dietary patterns following upon economic growth, they do not even mention the prospect that new demands on agricultural lands to produce liquid fuels may be forthcoming.

In one of its most influential studies during the last decade, the FAO estimated the demand for food and meat production to increase (in volume) by 49 and 85 per cent, respectively, by 2050 (compared to 2005/2007; Bruinsma 2009:5). Note that the frequently quoted FAO figure which states that food production needs to increase by 70 per cent by 2050 is expressed in value terms, not in volumes; it is the latter which is most relevant to my concern, the global competition for limited land areas.

Add to this the equally increasing demand for fibres and fuels, and the seriousness of land constraints should be clear. To deal with all of these conflicting demands, producers of agrofuel scenarios have used three different approaches to frame the discussion about global potential: forecasting, backcasting, and fantasies.

## Forecasting: how much agrofuel can be produced?

One frequently asked question is how much agrofuel can be produced globally. When reviewing the discussion around this issue, UNEP gives a surprisingly large span, 40 to 1,100 exajoules per year (a 28-fold difference), and then arbitrarily settles for somewhere below the middle of the range, 200–400 EJ (see Table 2.1). The reason for such a wide span is the varying assumptions and estimates that the underlying studies build on, and the scaling-up effect when such differences are extrapolated to the whole globe, and projected into the future.

The actual global supply of energy (from all sources) is approximately 500–600 EJ. The upper bound for biomass by 2050 in Table 2.1 – 1,100 EJ – is thus immensely optimistic, implying that twice the total available energy today could be coming from biomass alone, requiring a 23-fold increase of biomass energy (which was 48 EJ in 2005). UNEP's more modest assessment of the potential, 200–400 EJ, is still impressive, an increase by four to ten times of today's global production of agro-energy by 2050.

Estimating the biomass *potential* is only the first step when elaborating a scenario for the *actual* production of agrofuel. Against the background of the optimism informing the estimates of Table 2.1, agrofuel production scenarios could have been expected to yield equally exuberant pictures, but although there are such examples, mostly from the agrofuel industry and its consultants, more sombre scenarios dominate. Typical here is the FAO, which foresees fast growth of agrofuels but still of a more modest kind: agrofuel volumes will double by 2015, and then double again by 2030, going from 2 to 3 per cent of total liquid fuels (FAO 2008:44, based on the assumption that total transport fuels also will grow, albeit at a slower rate).

To sum up: these scenarios predict impressive growth rates for agrofuels, but still not enough to make a major impact on the dependency on fossil fuels. What we find, then, is a paradox: on the one hand, agrofuels are simply too small to

*Table 2.1* Global potential of biomass for energy, 2050, EJ/year

| Biomass source | Potential span | "Realistic" span |
| --- | --- | --- |
| Energy farming on current agricultural land | 0–700 | 100–300 |
| Biomass production on marginal land | 60–110 | – |
| Residues from agriculture | 15–70 | – |
| Forest residues | 30–150 | – |
| Dung | 5–55 | – |
| Organic wastes | 5–50 | – |
| **Total** | **40–1,100** | **200–400** |

Source: UNEP 2009:40.

Notes
EJ = exajoule = quintillion joules = billion billion joules.
Figures are for all energy uses of biomass, not only agrofuels.

play a leading part in the postulated metabolic regime shift from fossil to renewable energies; on the other hand, the expansion of agrofuel feedstocks will have important consequences by competing for land which already has other uses. The substitutability of land used for food, feed, fibres and fuels means that increasing agrofuel production will immediately impact other uses, leading to direct and indirect land-use change all along the supply chains.

### Backcasting: how much agrofuel is needed to meet blending requirements?

The second approach is in one sense more realistic, as it takes as its point of departure the mandatory blending requirements already decided. All over the world, in the South no less than in the North, such blending goals have been put in place: see Table 2.2.

The trend is global, with India mandating 20 per cent for both ethanol and biodiesel by 2017, and China 10 per cent (in nine provinces); but the most important mandates are the requirements of the US to sell 137 billion litres of agrofuels on the US domestic market by 2022, and the EU target of 10 per cent renewables in transport by 2020. Backcasting from such mandates, we arrive at the volumes that need to be produced somewhere on the globe; Table 2.3 investigates the consequences of a hypothetical global blending goal of 10 per cent by 2030.

The assumption underlying Table 2.3 – not very convincing – is that the total need will be supplied by one feedstock alone. But the results are nevertheless worth pondering: even a modest global blending requirement of 10 per cent would entail a very strong demand for agricultural land areas.

Are the land areas of Table 2.3 large or small? The answer depends on what you compare them to: compared to the crops in question they are very large indeed, but compared to the global crop area – 1.5 billion hectares – meeting a 10 per cent blending requirement does not seem an impossible proposition. Consider, for instance, using sugarcane to meet the total need: its land area has to increase by 350 per cent, not impossible given the rather small land area globally planted with sugarcane, 20 million hectares.

### Fantasies: what if we move people and agriculture around as we please?

Thinking about the future in this way – forecasting, backcasting – may be too cautious, however. In the light of the task set before us by "peak oil", we should ask the really dramatic question: "How much land do we need in order to do away with the global use of petrol?"

This is a tall order – remember that agrofuels today account for only 2 per cent of liquid fuel use – so we had better contemplate using all available feedstocks, irrespective of their yields, thus also including feedstocks that today normally are left out of the discussion because of their alternative use (such as wheat and rice). How much of today's petrol could then possibly be replaced by ethanol? See Table 2.4.

By using as much as 599 million hectares – 40 per cent of global crop land – we would still only replace 57 per cent of today's petrol use. But then *all* of the land areas dedicated to the world's major food crops – wheat, rice and maize – would be occupied by feedstocks for agrofuels, and the world's food needs

*Table 2.2* Current and future blending targets and mandates

| Country/region | Current target/mandate | Future target/mandate |
|---|---|---|
| Argentina | E5, B7 | – |
| Australia (New South Wales) | E6, B5 | – |
| Bolivia | E10, B2.5 | B20 (2015) |
| Brazil | E20–25, B5 | – |
| Canada | E5, B2 | – |
| Chile | E5, B5 | – |
| China (nine provinces) | E10 | |
| Colombia | E10, B20 | – |
| Costa Rica | E7, B20 | – |
| Dominican Republic | | E5, B2 (2015) |
| European Union | 5.75% biofuels | 10% renewable energy in transport (2020) |
| India | E5 | E20, B20 (2017) |
| Indonesia | E3, B2.5 | E5, B5 (2015); E15, B20 (2025) |
| Japan | 500 Ml/year | 800 Ml/year (2018) |
| Kenya (Kisumu) | E10 | – |
| Korea | B3 | – |
| Malaysia | B5 | – |
| Mexico (Guadalajara, Monterrey, Mexico City) | E2 | – |
| Mozambique | | E10, B15 (2015) |
| Norway | 3.5% biofuels | – |
| Nigeria | E10 | – |
| Paraguay | E24, B1 | – |
| Peru | E7.8, B5 | – |
| Philippines | E10, B5 | – |
| South Africa | | 2% (2013) |
| Taiwan | E3, B2 | – |
| Thailand | B5, 3 Ml/day ethanol | 9 Ml/day ethanol (2017) |
| Uruguay | B5 | E5 (2015) |
| USA | 48 Gl ethanol | 137 Gl ethanol (2022) |
| Venezuela | E10 | – |
| Vietnam | | 50 Ml biodiesel, 500 Ml ethanol (2020) |
| Zambia | E5, B10 | – |

Source: IEA 2011b, Table 1, and REN 2011.

Note
E=ethanol (E2=2% ethanol blend); B=biodiesel (B2=2% biodiesel blend); Ml=million litres, Gl=billion litres.

*Table 2.3* Land area required to meet global blending requirements of 10 per cent by
2030

|  | Palm oil | Soybean | Maize | Sugarcane | Sorghum |
|---|---|---|---|---|---|
| Land area needed, million hectares | 48 | 361 | 147 | 70 | 116 |
| Global crop land area today, million hectares | 41 | 91 | 145 | 20 | 45 |
| Percentage of today's land area required for agrofuels by 2030 | 117 | 396 | 101 | 350 | 258 |

Sources: Ravindranath *et al.* 2009:121, USDA 2009, and FAO 2008.

would have to be grown somewhere else, a clear fuel–food conflict caused by
the fungibility of land combined with limited land areas.

   Although scenarios such as this resemble far-fetched games, the truth is that
such fantasies are presented as serious, science-based inputs to the discussion of
the future energy system of the planet. Here, the so called scientific community
is playing a shady role, legitimating abstract thinking and encouraging that we
disregard potential conflicts related to large-scale transfers of land. Take the idea
that food production ought to be carried out where the preconditions are the best
globally. The reason for this mind game is that the actual food production pattern
today is seen as less than ideal, and researchers and think tanks suggest in
earnest a transfer of agricultural production from today's supposedly suboptimal
land areas to land where yields are higher. This means basically concentrating
food production to highly productive regions which are thought to be under-used
today (in this view, Russia and Eastern Europe are especially under-used), while
liberating less productive land from the need to produce food. In this scenario,
Africa, once relieved of the need to provide food crops to its population, is explicitly targeted as a future provider of agrofuel feedstocks.

*Table 2.4* Hypothetical ethanol potential and share of today's global petrol use

| Feedstock | Global land area today, million hectares | Potential ethanol production, billion litres | Share of global petrol use, % |
|---|---|---|---|
| Wheat | 215 | 205 | 12 |
| Rice | 150 | 271 | 16 |
| Maize | 145 | 284 | 17 |
| Sorghum | 45 | 22 | 1 |
| Sugarcane | 20 | 91 | 6 |
| Cassava | 19 | 39 | 2 |
| Sugar beet | 5 | 27 | 2 |
| **Total** | **599** | **939** | **57** |

Source: FAO 2008, Table 3.

Note
Total crop land is 1,500 Mha.

After such a transfer of agriculture from less productive to highly productive regions, the food production system would in theory attain a greatly increased area efficiency, and considerably less crop land would be needed. But I am understating the dramatic conclusion; note the result of one such fantasy that suggests global "optimization" of agriculture:

> Results indicated that the application of very efficient agricultural systems combined with the geographic optimization of land use patterns could reduce the area of land needed to cover the global food demand in 2050 by as much as 72 per cent of the present area.
>
> (Smeets *et al.* 2007:56)

The choice of words is not innocent. A total remake of global agricultural land use, presumably doing away with the food security and sovereignty of one to two billion people, is called "geographic optimization". And the land areas thus cleansed (my use of a loaded word) become in the following step "surplus agricultural land" (Smeets *et al.* 2007:56), a notion that holds out the promise that nobody will be hurt if over two-thirds of present agricultural lands are freed in order to be turned over to the production of agrofuel feedstocks.

In a similar study we are encouraged to do away with the "constraints on localizing agricultural production" that we have inherited from the past, to "think outside the box" and shift agricultural production to the land areas where productivity is highest; the approach taken is called "globalized production". The conclusion, just as in the previous study, is that the land areas needed to feed the planet could be substantially reduced. In this scenario, the land-saving potential is even higher – 85 per cent – as "globalized production" is calculated to only need 15 per cent of today's crop land to produce food for the whole planet; the remainder is thus vacant and could be made available for agrofuels, a truly stunning result (Müller *et al.* 2006:1 and Table 5).

Of course, people still have to eat, but this may be arranged by transporting food from the high-producing surplus to the deficit areas. That we are dealing with fantasies here is evident from the fact that the "globalized" land-use pattern is based on assuming "an unrestricted global market (no trade barriers, no transportation costs, no subsidies)" (Müller *et al.* 2006:5). But such unreal assumptions are needed if you are to construct a scenario where everybody's food as well as energy security is based on, and presupposes the possibility of, exchanges over large distances and across national borders.

Behind the term "globalized production" we find a redistribution of land use for the production of food, feed, fibres and fuels for a global market. Food will be produced in North America, Europe, and the former Soviet Union, while Africa and Latin America will concentrate on producing feedstocks for meat and agrofuels.

Although this scenario is called "global", it advocates concentration of food production to today's highly productive agricultural countries, thus offering a powerful resource weapon which, among other objectives, could be used to secure a continuous flow of agrofuels from the South. In case of non-compliance by feedstock producers such as Mozambique (sugarcane), Malaysia and Indonesia (palm oil), the food arm – the withholding of food exports to deficit countries – could be used to bring recalcitrant feedstock suppliers in line. In this way, these scenarios unexpectedly – considering their unreal assumptions – do show geopolitical realism by justifying displacing food production, and the power that goes with it, from the South to the North.

Global scenarios of this kind assume the existence of docile suppliers of feedstocks in exchange for food imports which they need to provide for their own populations. To repeat, such exercises are not innocent; they play an important role in legitimizing thinking (first) and acting (later) to secure the land areas and the land-based resources that powerful interests need in order to secure their own socio-ecological metabolism. Thus, to me, fantasies such as these are indications that the strategic interest in land areas is shifting.

The "scientific community" is obfuscating the geopolitical aspects arising from, and the power struggles surrounding, such grand transformations of land use. Instead, arguments and scenarios are frequently discussed as if there were no conflicts or contradictions in overcoming the global resource constraints of limited land areas and land-based resources. A case in point is the argument that was presented in the guise of a state-of-the art report to the Conference of the Parties (COP 15) at the UN Framework Convention on Climate Change in Copenhagen in 2009 (Richardson *et al.* 2009). The cover of this "synthesis report" presents an impressive list of the members of the International Alliance of Research Universities: Australian National University, ETH Zürich, National University of Singapore, Peking University, University of California at Berkeley, University of Cambridge, University of Copenhagen, University of Oxford, University of Tokyo, and Yale University.

In their report, there are no conflicts regarding climate change and climate policies which cannot be overcome if only politicians would listen more to scientists. The International Alliance of Research Universities claims:

> Science needs to demonstrate (i) what an "optimal" land-use pattern might look like; (ii) that this pattern would warrant the generation of sufficient quantities of the desired functions and resources; and (iii) which sociopolitical strategies can realise the envisioned transformation in good time.
> (quote from a contribution to Richardson *et al.* 2009:35 by Hans Joachim Schellnhuber and Veronika Huber of the Potsdam Institute for Climate Impact Research)

The "scientific community" labelled this approach "visionary" and expressed its wish to

> consider a novel global division of land-use activities that would significantly improve the geographical pattern of food and fibre production, biodiversity protection, infrastructure and energy generation.
> (Richardson *et al.* 2009:34)

Note the choice of words: science, optimal, functions, visionary, novel, improve. In fact, the "scientific community" has based its visionary ideas on the fantasies of researchers who dream of a world without history, without conflicts and contradictions over land, and without power struggles.

## Fantasy check: how many vegans can the Earth stomach?

Although scenarios of future agrofuel production are, as we have seen, typically based on extremely unrealistic assumptions, most of them nevertheless fear to enter the topic of dietary change: reducing meat consumption is an option which is left out of many of the scenarios considered.

Even when the importance of lifestyle changes is recognized in principle, such aspects are nevertheless not included in the "realistic" scenarios. Thus, in a state-of-the-art review of agrofuels and land availability, commissioned for the well-known *Gallagher Review*, the consultant simply skips the whole issue: "As we do not consider the vegetarian and affluent diets to be very realistic for 2020, we simply discarded these results in the analysis here" (CE Delft 2008:11–12). The international non-governmental organization Oxfam recently launched a campaign to cut hunger in the world without considering the varying demands on agricultural lands of different diets: the campaign recognized no conflicts in pitting meat consumption for the global middle and upper classes and agrofuels for their cars against the basic food rights of poor people, in spite of the fact that a reduction of meat or agrofuels could free large land areas for the production of food for millions of people. Oxfam does recognize that meat consumption appropriates much more water and space per kilo or calorie than grains, but nevertheless avoids the obvious conclusion from such well-known facts, preferring to stick to a traditional distributional perspective: if food was distributed equally, no-one would go hungry (Oxfam 2011a:66 and Figure 3). Perhaps Oxfam was simply afraid to play "the meat card" and take on powerful opponents in the global North, who can be assumed to cherish their right to eat meat and drive cars.

More daring scenarios may be devised when lifestyle changes are factored in: assuming more sustainable dietary patterns has dramatic consequences for land use, and hence for the availability of land, which in turn spills over to the question of potential conflicts over land (Wirsenius 2003; Hoogwijk *et al.* 2003; Müller *et al.* 2006; Erb *et al.* 2009a; Wirsenius *et al.* 2010; Foley *et al.* 2011). Meat is the crucial issue, as it has been estimated that 350 million hectares of today's crop lands are used to produce feed for animals, approximately one-fourth of the total cropped area (Foley *et al.* 2011:338).

I will present an attempt to measure the potential for agrofuels in a context of lifestyle changes. I take as my point of departure the forecasts for population growth and calorie development published by the relevant UN agencies, and then I look at what happens with the required land areas if we simultaneously change our food and feed production to the maximum area-efficient agriculture I have found in the North, a high-tech, mechanized, high-input system; see the Appendix to this chapter for details.

Since I am elaborating my scenarios in the context of the double peak for oil and soil, I use only the five billion hectares which already today are being cropped and grazed. After providing for food for the global human population in such an area-efficient production system, I then ask what land areas, if any, will be available for producing agrofuels.

From this it should be clear that I proceed in the opposite order from the one we came across in the previous scenarios: instead of focusing on the potential for producing agrofuel feedstocks, I will calculate the share of today's crop and pasture lands which could be made available for such feedstocks *after* discounting the areas required to meet global food needs. The results are presented in Table 2.5. The first two scenarios deal with the situation in 2010; the three following scenarios build on the assumed global population, calorie regimes and diets of 2050.

### Scenarios 1 and 2: year 2010

Would it mean a lot if we increased the land area efficiency? Yes, Scenario 1 shows that even with a wealthy diet – 35 per cent animal calories – there would still be 26 per cent of the agricultural land available for agrofuel production – 1.3 billion hectares – since the area needed for food and feed would be greatly reduced with area-efficient agriculture.

If we leave the wealthy diet and assume less animal consumption, still larger land areas would be freed up, 2.4 billion hectares and 3.9 billion hectares for sufficiency and vegan diets, respectively. These are very large land areas made available for other uses than producing food, feed and meat.

Even the assumption that everybody on Earth has a lifestyle heavy in calories – scenario 2 – would not alter the conclusion substantially: the available land areas would shrink, of course, but even a wealthy lifestyle would leave as much as 10 per cent of total crop and pasture lands – 500 million hectares – for agrofuels if it is area-efficiently produced.

### Scenarios 3, 4 and 5: year 2050

The remaining scenarios of Table 2.5 deal with the future: what happens by 2050 when the world population will be 9.1 billion people, with heavier diets on average.

- Can an average (3,130 kcal) or a heavy (3,540 kcal) and wealthy (35 per cent meat) diet be sustained on the available land areas by 2050? Scenario 3 and 4 indicate No.
- But what if we reduce our diets to sufficiency levels (i.e. only 20 per cent animal-based food)? Yes, then even a global population of 9.1 billion people will fit, leaving substantial lands – 1.2 or 0.7 billion hectares depending on the calorie intake – for agrofuels.
- With vegan diets, the land areas available would be much greater still, naturally: 3.4 or 3.2 billion hectares respectively, even despite the assumed larger calorie intakes of scenarios 3 and 4.

*Table 2.5* What if? Share of global crop and pasture land areas to satisfy human diets 2010 and 2050, percentages and billion hectares

| Scenario number and year | Lifestyle calories | Global population (millions) | Vegan diet | Sufficiency diet: 20% animal | Wealthy diet: 35% animal |
|---|---|---|---|---|---|
| 1: 2010 | with 2001 average diet (2,789 kcal) | 6,900 | 22% = 1.1 Gha | 52% = 2.6 Gha | 74% = 3.7 Gha |
| 2: 2010 | with 2001 heavy diet (3,446 kcal) | 6,900 | 26% = 1.3 Gha | 64% = 3.2 Gha | 90% = 4.5 Gha |
| 3: 2050 | with average diet (3,130 kcal) | 9,100 | 32% = 1.6 Gha | 76% = 3.8 Gha | 110% = 5.5 Gha |
| 4: 2050 | with heavy diet (3,540 kcal) | 9,100 | 36% = 1.8 Gha | 86% = 4.3 Gha | 124% = 6.2 Gha |
| 5: 2050 | with frugal diet (2,700 kcal) | 9,100 | 28% = 1.4 Gha | 66% = 3.3 Gha | 94% = 4.7 Gha |

Notes
See Appendix of Chapter 2 and Tables 2.7–2.12.
Globally available land area = 5 Gha, of which 1.5 Gha is crops and 3.5 Gha is pastures. Gha = giga ha = 1 billion ha.

In other words, to change to a less meaty diet is the easiest way to reconcile the conflicting demands on limited land resources arising from population increase and economic growth.

Changing to a less heavy diet in terms of calories would also liberate significant land areas, as shown in Scenario 5: with a frugal diet of 2,700 kcal per day, all lifestyles fit within the available areas.

### 33 billion vegans

Let's take the analysis one step further. What if every human being adopts a vegan lifestyle, how many people can today's agricultural land areas then support (assuming, as always, area-efficient agriculture, and upholding the limit of 5 billion hectares)? This is not a very realistic scenario, perhaps, but it does give food for thought:

- If we assume a heavy lifestyle (3,540 kcal per day, but still vegan), the global population which can be sustained on five billion hectares is 25 billion people.
- With a frugal vegan lifestyle (2,700 kcal per day), the agricultural and grazing land areas of this Earth can support as many as 33 billion people.

The calculus is quite simple: I divide the available land area – five billion hectares – with the area requirements of the various vegan lifestyles (see Appendix to this chapter). Thus, for a frugal lifestyle (2,700 kcal per day): five billion/0.1533 = 33 billion people; for heavy but still vegan lifestyle (3,540 kcal per day): five billion/0.2008 = 25 billion people. But though simple, the outcome of my back-of-the-envelope calculation is not very different from results gained through more elaborate and ambitious – though not more reliable – procedures. For instance, a thorough study (Hoogwijk *et al.* 2003) analyses three diets (vegetarian, moderate, affluent), three population prognoses (low, medium and high: 8.7, 9.4 and 11.3 billion people by 2050, respectively), and two agricultural production systems (low external inputs, high external inputs). The scenario which is closest to my scenarios 4 and 5 is the one with high-input agriculture and a vegetarian lifestyle: this scenario leaves room for 34 billion people if all the available five billion hectares are used. In other words, although more elaborate, the conclusion is almost identical to mine: 34 billion vegetarians compared to 33 billion vegans.

Thus, if we want to use large land areas for agrofuel production, we have three options: find new lands on which to grow feedstocks; hope for a technical breakthrough which would allow us to use second- or third-generation feedstocks (based on grasses or residues from forestry, or algae); or limit the share of animal products and reduce calorie intake.

One caveat is necessary here: land-area-efficient agriculture – one of the basic assumptions of my scenarios in Table 2.5 – is heavily dependent on fossil-based inputs, which implies that this type of agriculture, although efficient in terms of land areas, is highly inefficient when it comes to energy balance. Hence, although we may have resolved the conflict over land this way, we may at the same time unwittingly have reinforced climate change.

We must beware of interpreting these scenarios to mean that 9 billion people could live sustainably on Earth if only they cut down their meat rations and reduced their calorie intake; land areas are dedicated to many other purposes than food and feed, as we have seen. Although a lighter and less meaty diet would free up large land areas from food and meat production, lifestyle entails much more than food, and other resources may still constitute limiting factors. Deforestation to make room for plantations (e.g. eucalyptus) is likely to continue because of increasing demand for paper, just to take one land-based resource demand which is set to grow considerably; and water is already a constraint in many locations. In addition, a growing global population will take ever more land – frequently of the most fertile kind – for the construction of housing and transport infrastructure, thereby in fact reducing the land areas available to produce food, feed, fibres and fuels.

Of course, the basic underlying assumption of all of these scenarios is completely unrealistic: that all five billion hectares of today's crop and pasture lands are equally suitable for growing food. Obviously, this assumption is false. My scenarios should not, however, be seen in the light of realism, but rather as a way to question the framing of agrofuels scenarios which are presented in all seriousness by most attempts to model future socio-ecological metabolic profiles.

## Concluding remarks

Speculating about the number of people that the Earth can support is by no means a new undertaking: a survey lists over 65 historical assessments of the Earth's carrying capacity (Cohen 1995:212–215 and Appendix 3). The earliest one listed, by the Dutch scientist Antoni van Leeuwenhoek in 1679, considered the limit for the global population to be 13.4 billion people, a figure which sounds surprisingly contemporary. In fact, the estimates over the centuries show no trend: early scenarios are of a similar magnitude to later ones, with the most frequent range for the maximum global population set at 8–16 billion people. My outcome – a vegan population of 25–33 billion people – thus falls in the upper segment of the continuum of estimates of the past three centuries.

Should such scenarios be taken seriously? Yes, I believe so, and for two reasons. First, they serve as an antidote to the fanciful imaginings which we came across earlier in this chapter: it should be recognized that scenarios are no more reliable than the assumptions on which they are built. Although the scenarios of Table 2.5 admittedly are more simplistic than most, they nevertheless capture the essential contradiction in relation to land use: land conflicts do not arise because there are too many people on this planet, but because we are living with a particular socio-ecological metabolism which requires a continuous supply of land-based resources for food, feed, fibres and fuels.

Not all people on the planet contribute equally to the conflict over land-based resources, of course: a person's responsibility for the emissions of greenhouse

*Table 2.6* Differences in metabolic profiles, *c.*2000

|  | South | North |
|---|---|---|
| Electricity per capita (joules) | 1 | 10 |
| Gross domestic product per capita (USD) | 1 | 6 |
| Energy use per capita (joules) | 1 | 4 |
| Material use per capita (tons) | 1 | 3 |
| Animal-based diet per capita (joules) | 1 | 3 |

Source: Based on Krausmann *et al.* 2008, Table 3.
Notes
South=Africa, Asia (excluding Japan), Latin America, Oceania (excluding Australia and New Zealand).
North=Europe, North America, Japan, Australia and New Zealand.

gases, for instance, is closely related to his or her class position in the global system as well as to personal lifestyle choices. A rich man is simply a greater predator in terms of his impact on climate and land areas than a poor woman. And so is an omnivorous person compared to a vegetarian. In fact, carbon footprints closely follow class as well as gender: rich people and men constitute more of a problem than poor people and women (Swedish EPA 2008:41).

But in addition to wealth, gender, and personal choice of lifestyle, the global position of the society in which we live is equally significant for the footprint we impose on land areas and land-based resources. Unsurprisingly, societies of the North are using three to ten times the resources used by the societies of the South, per capita: see Table 2.6.

Secondly, such scenarios are important as part of a raging battle concerning how to frame the discourse on resource limits. Fanciful scenarios, built on unrealistic assumptions, contribute arguments regarding how conflicts over land areas and land-based resources can be dissolved. Behind these scenarios we find not only academic researchers but also corporations, consultancy firms, international organizations, and financial institutions, and they all take sides one way or the other through the futures they commission, elaborate or disseminate.

Nevertheless, playing mind games may aid us in foreseeing the consequences of an ever fiercer struggle over land. Judging by the historically high price levels of food and raw materials (as shown in Figure 2.1) amidst on-going financial and economic crises, it seems likely that struggles over land will intensify. One of the countries where such land competition will play itself out is Brazil, the world's second most important producer of ethanol and soybeans (next to the US). This is the topic of the following chapter.

# Appendix

## *Data and assumptions for calculating land use for different diets*

The scenarios of Table 2.5 above are built on the following assumptions (FAO 2006, Peters *et al.* 2007, Lundqvist *et al.* 2007).

- Land for crops and pasture is fixed at today's five billion hectares, which amounts to assuming no deforestation and no use of "abandoned" or "degraded" lands.
- The agricultural system will be a high-intensive, land-area-efficient farm system such as that found in New York State.
- All pastures can be transformed into high-yielding crop lands.

I measure lifestyles in terms of their daily calorie intake, as estimated by the FAO, and calculate the land areas needed to provide for each lifestyle.

*Assumed calorie intake (kilocalories per capita per day)*

- Global average today (2001): 2,789 kcal
- Heavy lifestyle today (2001): 3,446 kcal
- Global average prognosis (2050): 3,130 kcal
- Heavy lifestyle prognosis (2050): 3,540 kcal
- Frugal: 2,700 kcal

Then I combine the "heaviness" of the lifestyle, i.e. its calorie intake, with the share of animal products in the diet. Three diets are investigated:

- a wealthy lifestyle, defined by its large share of meat: 35 per cent animal calories, equal to rich countries' average meat share today;
- a "sufficiency" lifestyle, 20 per cent animal calories;
- a vegan lifestyle.

*Composition of diets*

- Vegan: 50 per cent grains, 50 per cent remaining plant products with equal weights.
- Omnivorous: plant products as vegans, plus 20 or 35 per cent meat (unweighed average consumption of animal products in Table 2.7).

*Population*

The population prognosis used here for 2050 is 9.1 billion people (UN 2009, median scenario). In the most recent population update (UN 2011:2), the 2050 medium variant is 9.3 billion, with global population levelling out at 10.1 billion by 2100. My scenarios thus err on the optimistic side by using a lower population figure.

*Agricultural production system*

The calculation is based on an area-efficient, rich-country model (high input/ high output model, high land area efficiency) based on data for New York State (see Table 2.7).

*Table 2.7* Land area required per 1,000 kcal of various foods

|  |  | $m^2/1,000\,kcal$ |
| --- | --- | --- |
| Animal products | Beef | 31.2 |
|  | Chicken | 9.0 |
|  | Pork | 7.3 |
|  | Eggs | 6.0 |
|  | Milk | 7.0 |
| Plant products | Oils | 3.2 |
|  | Fruits | 2.3 |
|  | Pulses | 2.2 |
|  | Vegetables | 1.7 |
|  | Grains | 1.1 |
|  | Sugar | 0.6 |

Sources: Peters *et al.* 2007, and WBGU 2009:66.

Note
Each animal product's area has been calculated according to estimated feeding quotas, for instance for beef: 0.85 ha pasture, 2.4 tons hay, 1.7 tons corn, 68 kg soy; for pork: 70% maize, 23% soy and 7% minerals plus 3 kg of ration per kg of weight gained.

## Total land area requirement per thousand kilocalories per day and year (Tables 2.8–2.12)

* Animal products diet:
  12.1 m²/1,000 kcal per day;
  4,417 m²/1,000 kcal per year.
* Plant products diet:
  1.55 m²/1,000 kcal per day;
  566 m²/1,000 kcal per year.

*Table 2.8* Land area required for diets of 2,789 kcal/day/capita (2001 global average)

| Diet | Animal products, m²/capita/ day | Animal products, ha/capita/ year | Plant products, m²/capita/ day | Plant products, ha/capita/ year | Total land area, m²/capita/ day | Total land area, ha/capita/ year |
| --- | --- | --- | --- | --- | --- | --- |
| Vegan | 0 | 0 | 4.3 | 0.1570 | 4.3 | 0.1570 |
| 20% animal | 6.8 | 0.2482 | 3.5 | 0.1278 | 10.3 | 0.3760 |
| 35% animal | 11.8 | 0.4307 | 2.8 | 0.1022 | 14.6 | 0.5329 |

*Table 2.9* Land area required for diets of 3,446 kcal/day/capita (2001 wealthy diet)

| Diet | Animal products, $m^2$/capita/day | Animal products, ha/capita/year | Plant products, $m^2$/capita/day | Plant products, ha/capita/year | Total land area, $m^2$/capita/day | Total land area, ha/capita/year |
|---|---|---|---|---|---|---|
| Vegan | 0 | 0 | 5.3 | 0.1935 | 5.3 | 0.1935 |
| 20% animal | 8.3 | 0.3030 | 4.3 | 0.1570 | 12.6 | 0.4539 |
| 35% animal | 14.6 | 0.5329 | 3.5 | 0.1278 | 18.1 | 0.6607 |

*Table 2.10* Land area required for diets of 3,130 kcal/day/capita (2050 global average)

| Diet | Animal products, $m^2$/capita/day | Animal products, ha/capita/year | Plant products, $m^2$/capita/day | Plant products, ha/capita/year | Total land area, $m^2$/capita/day | Total land area, ha/capita/year |
|---|---|---|---|---|---|---|
| Vegan | 0 | 0 | 4.9 | 0.1789 | 4.9 | 0.1789 |
| 20% animal | 7.6 | 0.2774 | 3.9 | 0.1424 | 11.5 | 0.4198 |
| 35% animal | 13.3 | 0.4855 | 3.2 | 0.1168 | 16.5 | 0.6023 |

*Table 2.11* Land area required for diets of 3,540 kcal/day/capita (2050 wealthy diet)

| Diet | Animal products, $m^2$/capita/day | Animal products, ha/capita/year | Plant products, $m^2$/capita/day | Plant products, ha/capita/year | Total land area, $m^2$/capita/day | Total land area, ha/capita/year |
|---|---|---|---|---|---|---|
| Vegan | 0 | 0 | 5.5 | 0.2008 | 5.5 | 0.2008 |
| 20% animal | 8.6 | 0.3139 | 4.4 | 0.1606 | 13.0 | 0.4745 |
| 35% animal | 15.0 | 0.5475 | 3.6 | 0.1314 | 18.6 | 0.6789 |

*Table 2.12* Land area required for diets of 2,700 kcal/day/capita (sufficiency norm)

| Diet | Animal products, $m^2$/capita/day | Animal products, ha/capita/year | Plant products, $m^2$/capita/day | Plant products, ha/capita/year | Total land area, $m^2$/capita/day | Total land area, ha/capita/year |
|---|---|---|---|---|---|---|
| Vegan | 0 | 0 | 4.2 | 0.1533 | 4.2 | 0.1533 |
| 20% animal | 6.5 | 0.2373 | 3.3 | 0.1205 | 9.8 | 0.3577 |
| 35% animal | 11.4 | 0.4161 | 2.7 | 0.0986 | 14.1 | 0.5147 |

Note
Totals may not match due to rounding.

# 3 Regulating land use for agrofuels
## The case of Brazil

The sugarcane-ethanol complex in Brazil is governed by a series of codes, regulations and agreements covering how and where sugarcane is grown and harvested. This regulatory set-up includes the Brazilian forest code and voluntary agreements between the state, the sugarcane industry, and the labour unions, as well as conditions for entering the EU and US markets.

This chapter is based on field-work and interviews that I conducted in the autumn of 2010 in the states of Goiás and São Paulo (Figure 3.1 shows a sugarcane field in São Paulo). The interviewees are listed at the end of the chapter.

*Figure 3.1* Sugarcane field treated with the Monsanto herbicide Roundup after six harvests, ready for replanting, at sugar plantation Ester, Cosmópolis, São Paulo; the forested stretches along the waterways in the distance may be Areas for Permanent Preservation, APPs (author's photograph).

## The "tragedy of the commons" re-examined

Anyone who starts to ponder over the best way to regulate land use will sooner or later – probably sooner – come across the acrimonious debate between ecologist Garrett Hardin and political scientist Elinor Ostrom concerning "the tragedy of the commons". The phrase was used by Hardin in his influential article of 1968, where he argued against population growth in terms not very different from the ones that Malthus had used 170 years earlier. Hardin concurs with Malthus that population "naturally tends to grow 'geometrically', or as we would now say, exponentially", we live in a finite world, and a "finite world can support only a finite population; therefore, population growth must eventually equal zero" (Hardin 1968:1243).

Exponential population growth will clash with the limits of land areas and other restricting resources, Hardin postulated, taking as his case a common pasture. While each of the "rational herdsmen" is following his own profit-maximizing path by augmenting his own herd, the outcome spells ruin for all:

> Therein is the tragedy. Each man is locked into a system that compels him to increase his herd without limit – in a world that is limited. Ruin is the destination toward which all men rush, each pursuing his own best interest in a society that believes in the freedom of the commons. Freedom in a commons brings ruin to all.
>
> (Hardin 1968:1244)

The tragedy, Hardin held, was fed by the erroneous ideas of Adam Smith that there existed an "invisible hand" which turned individual profit-maximization into a public good, thereby justifying "the continuance of our present policy of laissez-faire in reproduction" (Hardin 1968:1244). To deal with this tragedy, Hardin most of all wanted to restrict population growth by "reveal[ing] to all the necessity of abandoning the freedom to breed" (Hardin 1968:1248) – a position which brings him quite close to the first version of Malthus's essay.

But it is Hardin's favouring of the privatization of common resources which has been targeted by his foes, although Hardin in fact did make an interesting distinction – usually disregarded when assessing his position – between commons that were best governed by private ownership, and those that needed state regulation. Hardin believed in private property to protect land against overuse, but not when the issue was pollution. Pollution, unlike land, could not be governed easily by private owners, since "the air and waters surrounding us cannot readily be fenced". What was needed here, Hardin maintained, was state action, "coercive codes or taxing devices" to make the polluter change his ways (Hardin 1968:1245).

Thus Hardin recognized two alternatives for managing common land resources, privatization or state regulation, and he mostly preferred the former to the latter. Elinor Ostrom objected to Hardin's dichotomy and made the point that there existed many different – albeit variously effective – governance systems for common resources, not just a sterile polarization between two extreme options.

Hardin later appeared to retreat from his first provocative formulation when he "revisited" the debate 30 years after the publication of his original piece. He then recognized that he ought to have called it "the tragedy of the *unmanaged commons*", a position which at first appears to bring Hardin quite close to Ostrom's stance. But he still accepted only two regimes, even for "managed" commons: "A 'managed commons' describes either socialism or the privatism of free enterprise. Either one may work, either one may fail" (Hardin 1998:683). From this we see that Hardin never overcame his binary thinking, either-or; but he did not believe exclusively in privatization, although this is how he is usually understood. In fact, he also recognized a role for state regulation.

Ostrom's argument is also limited in a way that makes her famous case less relevant to the actual situation we find on the ground in Brazil. On the one hand, she is correct in arguing that it is usual for the kind of abstract reasoning that Hardin exemplifies to be based on "idealized markets or idealized states" (Ostrom 1990:216). This is no empty objection: Hardin's argument is totally free of any empirical basis – he just assumes the situation he "analyzes". Ostrom's account, on the other hand, is based on case studies, from which she deducts general rules of understanding of what works, and what does not, when it comes to governing common resources. The official motivation for awarding Ostrom the Nobel Prize in Economics in 2009 sums up her position neatly:

> based on numerous empirical studies of natural-resource management, Elinor Ostrom has concluded that common property is often surprisingly well managed. Thus, the standard theoretical argument against common property is overly simplistic. It neglects the fact that users themselves can both create and enforce rules that mitigate overexploitation. The standard argument also neglects the practical difficulties associated with privatization and government regulation.
>
> (Royal Swedish Academy of Sciences 2009:1)

On the other hand, this perspective, insightful as it is, is nevertheless best applicable to instances where "the users can substantially harm one another, but not situations in which participants can produce major external harm for others" (Ostrom 1990:26). This restriction in Ostrom's perspective is frequently overlooked, but for my Brazilian case study it will soon become clear that we need a much more complex understanding in order to govern the large number of national and international actors involved. Brazilian sugarcane ethanol is precisely a case where "major external harm for others" is frequent: the land-use change taking place as a consequence of the expansion of sugarcane cultivation occurs not only locally but also regionally, nationally and indeed globally. As land is fungible, land-use change is also a global process.

So, while the scale of Ostrom's perspective is restricted to local and perhaps regional settings, land-use change and land-use regimes need to be seen in a much wider context, from the national to the global. Ostrom's much celebrated perspective thus gives us less reason for hope than is customarily recognized.

Central to my concern regarding land use and land-use change is that regulations cannot be limited to a question of who has access to what common good, and who can block the access for whom; equally essential to the possibility of entering the global market is the performance of feedstocks all along the production chain in terms of a number of concerns, from labour conditions to carbon emissions and biological diversity.

In fact, a precondition for Brazilian sugarcane ethanol to be acceptable to major importers – states as well as corporations – is that it qualifies in all of these respects, a *sine qua non* for its being acknowledged as a sustainable alternative in the global hunt for substitutes to fossil fuels.

## Working the sugarcane fields

The way the sugarcane sector in Brazil is depicted by the sugarcane industry is seductive: clean, carbon neutral, geopolitically secure, without ecological drawbacks, the ideal raw material for fuelling the world's automobiles. As we are led to understand in a recent publication by the União Nacional da Indústria de Cana-de-açúcar (UNICA, the sugarcane industry association in São Paulo, which is the Brazilian ethanol industry's leading lobby group), ethanol is socially beneficial in that it creates jobs and wealth in the countryside and simultaneously improves Brazil's income distribution (UNICA 2009:8).

However, even a cursory visit to a sugarcane district during harvest time will disclose a completely different picture, at least where manual labour still is essential: the cutting of the sugarcane is arduous, dirty and hazardous work, and the living conditions of the workforce are degrading. It does not help that the ecological consequences are also dubious, especially when new land is cleared for sugarcane and when it comes to its impact on biodiversity.

All sugarcane that is cut manually is first burned on the preceding night, in order to facilitate the cutting and eliminate the parts of the cane which are useless for sugar production. In this way, productivity is increased, but so are pulmonary infections and diseases, not only for people directly involved in the cutting but also those living in the vicinity of the sugarcane fields, or in urban settlements nearby; the frequency of reported pulmonary problems almost doubles during the burning season in Ribeirão Preto, São Paulo, one of the prime sugarcane regions of Brazil (Silva 2010, Silva and Ribeiro 2010).

Several hundred thousand workers are employed as cane cutters during the harvesting season, from April to October (see Figure 3.2). The majority are young men under 30 years of age. Many are migrants from the northeast of Brazil; others live in the vicinity of the sugarcane plantations. Approximately 10 per cent of the cane cutters are women.

The average production load has increased substantially over the decades. Today, 12 tons per worker per day is held up as norm in a race towards ever higher performance; in the 1950s average daily production was three tons, and in the 1960s six tons. According to measurements of average work days, this is the day of a cane cutter: he/she walks 8,800 metres, bends down and strikes close to

*Figure 3.2* Female cane cutter in the smoking field, Denusa plantation, Indiára, Goiás (author's photograph).

the ground with his/her machete 133,332 times, makes 36,630 rotations of his/ her spine, loses eight litres of sweat. He/she carries the 12 tons of sugarcane in 800 instalments of 15 kilos each, and arranges them in easily measured lines (Alves 2006).

The only work tool is the machete, which the cutter sharpens and adapts to his/her own cutting technique. On the sugarcane plantations that I visited, most of the minimum required safeguards were followed (protective equipment, bus transport, lunch breaks in the shade), exceptional cases if we are to go by most studies of the dreadful working conditions of cane cutters (see Box 3.1).

---

**Box 3.1  Regulating manual cane cutting**

A combination of legally binding and voluntary rules and regulations establishes the conditions for manual labourers on Brazilian sugarcane plantations (Compromisso nacional 2009, Convenção coletiva 2010, NR 31 [Regulatory Norm 31] 2005, Protocolo de cooperação 2007).

**Code prohibiting slave labour**: Article 149 of the Brazilian penal code "Reduction of conditions analogous to slavery" metes out a punishment of two to eight years' imprisonment for anyone who enforces compulsion, exhausting working days, or degrading working conditions, or who limits the possibility for indebted employees to leave their employment. The Ministry of Labour provides a website where violators of this code are listed (www.reporterbrasil.org.br/pacto/listasuja/lista). In December 2012, 385 corporations were on the "dirty list" (Lista suja) for violating this agreement. Corporations and farms on the list are blocked from federal public finance, and some private banks follow suit.

**Regulatory Norm 31**: A national norm regarding "Safety and Health in Agricultural Work" was adopted in 2005. The cane cutter in Figure 3.2 wears gloves, glasses, shirt, boots and leg protection, all part of what Norm 31 stipulates, in addition to her non-regulatory hat. However, she does not use the facemask that she needs to protect herself from the smoke.

**Collective agreements**: Collective labour agreements for the sugarcane sector stipulate how salaries are paid, piece rates for different qualities of sugarcane, working hours and working days, the right to safety protection (and other rules of Regulatory Norm 31), and the right to leave-of-absence for menstruating women (without remuneration).

**Voluntary agreements**: A voluntary agreement to mechanize the harvesting of sugarcane in the state of São Paulo by 2014 has been signed between the state government and UNICA (for land with slopes less than 12 degrees). The agreement is more demanding than the national regulation, which stipulates full mechanization only by 2021. For slopes over 12 degrees, the deadline for mechanization is 2017 in São Paulo (as compared to the national goal of 2031).

**A national agreement to improve labour conditions** was concluded in 2009 between trade unions, the sugarcane industry, and the federal government to secure "decent work and quality of life" for workers on the sugarcane plantations. The agreement explicitly refers to Norm 31, but also prohibits the use by the employers of middlemen (gatos) who often trick migrating cane cutters into debt on their way to work, a prohibition which also is part of collective agreements.

Accidents caused by stress, exhaustion and over-exploitation are common; workers' heartbeat in the sun is exceedingly high, as is the overall strain. More than 20 workers are reported to have died in the fields or from being overworked from 2004 to 2007 (Rede Social de Justiça e Direitos Humanos 2008).

"Slave labour" – that is, workers suffering from slave-like conditions – is reported in appallingly many instances: for the whole of Brazil on average 6,000–7,000 workers were liberated *each year* from 2005 to 2009, half of them on sugarcane plantations. During the same period, approximately 30 people were killed *each year* in local struggles, and numerous conflicts about access to and ownership of land occurred, involving an average of 750,000 people *each year* (CPT 2010:16, 173). These struggles take place all over Brazil; there are no exceptions for "modern" or "developed" regions – São Paulo, for instance – as compared to the poorer areas in the northeast. A much-reported case of slave labour included Cosan, the leading sugarcane corporation in Brazil, which has Shell as one of its major partners (Mendonça 2010). Cosan blamed its recruiter of labour (the "gato") for the slave conditions of the workers; but according to both national and collective agreements to which Cosan is party, no middlemen are allowed in the recruitment of workers. The practice continues, however, and "gatos" now advertise "Excursions to São Paulo" since open recruitment is no longer permitted (interview with Maria Luisa Mendonça).

Pay is according to a piece-rate system by tons cut, but the foremen go by the metres cut of five rows ("linhas") of sugarcane (see Figures 3.3 and 3.4). The minimum monthly pay in Brazil in 2010 was 510 reais (US$300), and a cane cutter could earn twice that or more during the months of the cane harvest. On a yearly basis, however, the pay is not impressive, even for Brazilian conditions.

All in all, although there are good intentions on the legal as well as the voluntary level, the reality is still extremely exploitative. The average "useful" life of a manual cane cutter is only 15 years, which makes his or her working life in the sugarcane fields shorter than during the times of slavery in Brazil, where slaves lasted 20 years (Silva and Ribeiro 2010:3). Exceptions exist, especially in the macho culture of cane cutters (see Figure 3.5). For example, a trade union representative told me he had cut sugarcane for 20 years and managed 12 tons per day (interview with Valdemar Garrido). This level of production may earn the cutter

*Figure 3.3* The cutters' performance is measured and registered by the foreman; Plantation Ester, Cosmópolis, São Paulo (author's photograph).

*Figure 3.4* Sugarcane field after burning and cutting, with the burned and cut cane, ordered in "linhas", ready for transport to the mill; Plantation Denusa, Indiara, Goiás (author's photograph).

*Figure 3.5* Cane cutter Paulo Panceroli, 61 years old, who has been cutting cane for over 50 years: "Cane cutting kills nobody, otherwise I'd be dead by now"; Plantation Ester, Cosmópolis, São Paulo (author's photograph).

the "padão de ouro" (golden machete) premium – sometimes amounting to a motorbike, more frequently "uma cesta básica", one basic food ration (interview with Antônio Canuto and Isolete Widriweski).

## The future: better working conditions, fewer jobs

The trend towards mechanized harvesting will change most of this and push the attention relating to sugarcane ethanol towards its ecological dimension at the expense of the situation of the work force. Already today, approximately half the sugarcane harvest is mechanized (see Figures 3.6–3.8), with higher rates in the southeast and central west, and lower in the northeast. Surprisingly, there has been a movement to stop mechanization, or at least to slow it down. With this purpose, a law was proposed in 2008 at the state parliament of Goiás in order to limit mechanization to 50 per cent of the area of any plantation until 2020, and to 70 per cent by 2030. In other words, 30 per cent of the harvesting was to continue to take place manually, at least for the coming generation (Projeto de Lei 2008, backed by a member of the Partido Democrático Trabalhista, part of the ruling Partido dos Trabalhadores alliance).

The concern here, obviously, is employment, which the proposed code wants to protect. No mention is made in the proposal of working conditions or health problems related to manual cane cutting. Recalcitrant sugarcane plantations and trade unions, opposing the mechanization of harvesting, will have to conform to the overall trend, however; the "market" will not permit continued burning and manual cutting (interview with Eduardo Assad). And indeed, although manual labour can be expected to continue on the plantations with lands less suitable for mechanization – for instance, farms with steep slopes, stony grounds, or land areas with difficult access – as well as for the (primarily female) task of picking up what the harvesters miss to collect, called "bituca", mechanization is being introduced on ever more plantations.

Mechanization is most frequently presented as a result of demands from overseas markets which do not accept that a supposedly clean agrofuel is produced under slave-like conditions reminiscent of the sixteenth century. Domestic actors follow suit, for instance the public energy company Petrobras, and the days of large-scale burning may well be numbered, as mechanized harvesting does without it.

But although such pressure may constitute the main driver, there also exist other factors that have contributed to this shift. One is the profit motive: a harvester replaces 80–100 workers, and the average cost per ton harvested is almost halved (interview with Fábio Alves de Moura). Another factor pushing in the same direction has been conflicts on the plantations as workers' resistance to the dire conditions has taken various forms, from strikes to actions that will decrease the yield of the mill without endangering their own pay. For instance, small-scale obstruction (called "resistência miuda") can consist of hiding uncut sugarcane below the heaps of cut cane that the workers gather for transport to the mill, or by cutting too high above the ground so as to gain speed and save strength;

*Figures 3.6* Mechanized harvesting at Jalles Machado, Goianêsia, Goiás (author's photographs).

since the pay is according to metres cut, only the factory owner will suffer (Moraes 2007; Alves 2006; Silva 2008:21; Silva and Ribeiro 2010:7–8; interview with Maria Aparecida de Moraes Silva).

The fact that the children of today's cane cutters prefer to stay away from the sugarcane fields and aspire to find employment elsewhere, rather than being subjected to the degrading working conditions on the plantations, has also pushed the sugar and ethanol industry in the direction of mechanization (Plancherel *et al.* undated; Assad de Ávila *et al.* 2010; interviews with Mário Ávila, Silvia Assad de Ávila and Maria Aparecida de Moraes Silva). It has simply become difficult to find willing workers in sufficient numbers.

However, although mechanized harvesting would do away with some of the worst traits of manual cane cutting by eliminating most of the cutters, there are also problems related to mechanization, especially when it comes to its environmental consequences. Land will be more compacted, which increases water and wind erosion; and "efficient" mechanization requires that there are no obstacles in or along the fields, leading to the cultivation of large open and monotonous tracts of land and further endangering biodiversity, although the termination of burning may enhance it (interview with José Paulo Pietrafesa).

## Brazil's forest codes

The Brazilian forest code, as it stands today, puts quite far-reaching demands on private property owners, who must set aside two separate land areas for preservation and to protect biodiversity: a Legal Reserve (Reserva Legal, RL) and an Area for Permanent Preservation (Área de Preservação Permanente, APP).

The specifications for Legal Reserves vary among the biomes of Brazil (see Figure 3.7):

- In the Amazon, 80 per cent of private property holdings are to be set aside.
- For the Cerrado biome, a Savannah-like ecosystem, the RL share is 35 per cent within the Legal Amazon.
- For the remainder of the Brazilian territory, the RL is meant to be 20 per cent. This lower requirement also applies to the Cerrado outside of the Legal Amazon.

The Areas of Permanent Preservation are stipulated in metres on each side of water bodies (rivers and lakes), and the requirements depend on the width of the river: 30 metres of APP for rivers 10 m wide, 50 m for rivers 10–50 m wide, 100 m for rivers 50–200 m wide, 200 m for rivers 200–600 m wide, and 500 m for rivers wider than 600 m. The Areas of Permanent Preservation are also meant to include steep slopes, hilltops, and high altitudes (more than 1,800 m above sea level).

The forest code can be seen as an attempt to protect biodiversity in sensitive land areas (especially the Amazon) and in connection with water bodies, while also fighting erosion and protecting the water cycle. Here, the conservationist

*Figure 3.7* Brazilian vegetation zones (biomes), *c*.1500 (source: Instituto Brasileiro de
Geografia e Estatística, www.ibge.gov.br; used with permission). In Brazil, a
distinction is made between the state of Amazon (Amazonas), the Amazon
biome (Amazônia), and the Legal Amazon (Amazônia Legal). The Amazon
biome covers 49 per cent of Brazil's territory, including all of the states of
Acre, Amapá, Amazonas, Pará and Roraima, and parts of Rondônia (98 per
cent), Mato Grosso (54 per cent), Maranhão (34 per cent), and Tocantins (9
per cent). The Legal Amazon is the *totality* of all the states which harbour the
Amazon biome, except Maranhão which has part of its land area outside; the
Legal Amazon equals 61 per cent of Brazil's territory.

perspective is seen as more important than economic concerns. At the same time,
the code partly liberates other land areas for economic exploitation (to use the
term for economic activities suggested by the Convention on Biological Diversity), which is obvious from the varying requirements that it applies to the different Brazilian biomes, most importantly the Cerrado (inside as well as outside the
Legal Amazon; the Cerrado was largely intact at the time of the code, while
some of the other biomes already had been seriously damaged).

## Assessing the Brazilian forest code at different scales

Although the forest code has in no way stopped the deforestation taking place in Brazil, it has had an influence on where and how it has evolved. A certain slowing down of deforestation in the Amazon has been noticed during the last couple of years: while the annual deforestation recorded in the 1980s was two million hectares/year, it has since been much reduced, and by 2010 and 2011 it was down to 660,000 hectares (Sawyer 2009:150; INPE 2009, 2011). Deforestation in the Cerrado also continues, although with much less international attention: 760,000 hectares were cleared in 2008–2009, also down from an estimated annual rate of two million hectares (Embrapa 2008:10; Fischer *et al.* 2008:42).

Although the Amazon is regarded as containing the world's richest biodiversity resources, it is the Cerrado which has been named one of 25 global "biodiversity hotspots" on account of its high biodiversity density in combination with the threats that it is facing (Myers *et al.* 2000). However, all in all, deforestation in the Amazon may be considered to carry more drawbacks in terms of release of climate gases per hectare and loss of biodiversity, but that certainly should not be taken to imply that the continuing deforestation of the Cerrado is acceptable.

The deforestation frontier is now centred on the Cerrado as much as on the Amazon, and the total deforestation in the Cerrado has advanced more than in the Amazon, both in absolute and in relative terms. While the Amazon is estimated to have lost approximately 70 million hectares (or 20 per cent of its total land area), the Cerrado had by 2008 suffered a loss of 98 million hectares (or 48 per cent of its total land area; Bustamente *et al.* undated). From being the dominant land cover in large parts of Brazil (see Figure 3.7), the Cerrado – today high-valued land – has been turned into a seriously weakened biome.

Another way to evaluate the forest code is to measure the degree of compliance with the required Legal Reserves and Areas of Permanent Preservation, and here the verdict is still more damning. A recent assessment concludes that "the legal frameworks do not effectively achieve the objectives of protecting water and native vegetation on private farmland in Brazil" (Sparovek *et al.* 2010b:6050). The basis for this strong conclusion is that a large part of the land that should be set aside for biodiversity and conservation purposes in fact does not appear as Legal Reserve or Areas for Permanent Preservation. Out of the 233 million hectares of Legal Reserves theoretically required, at least 42 million hectares cannot be found; and of the 100 million hectares required for the APPs, at least 43 million hectares were not to be detected (Sparovek *et al.* 2010a:5). In other words, assessed in relation to its objective, the forest code has been a gigantic failure.

This is not a new understanding of the ineffectiveness of the code. Based on information on the forest cover back in 1996, it was shown that most Brazilian states did not have enough forested areas to comply with the requirements of the code: *none* of the states of the Legal Amazon had sufficient forest cover left, and even the more lenient demand of 20 per cent Legal Reserve could only be found in 13 out of 21 states, which means that eight states did not even have this more limited protection (Alston and Mueller 2007:37–38; the APPs were not measured in this study).

## The 1999/2012 forest code

A reformulated forest code has been a contentious issue ever since it was first proposed in 1999 (Câmara dos Deputados 1999). It has been called the "chain saw code" ("lei motoserra"), which gives an idea of how the critics view it: a sell-out and an end to the protection of land areas and the preservation of biological diversity in Brazil (Cruz 2010, FASE 2008). In a similar reaction, the Brazilian Academy of Sciences and the Brazilian Society for the Advancement of Science have issued a joint statement to the effect that the proposal was being framed "by stakeholders who would irreversibly hurt our natural ecosystems and the environmental services they perform" (Brazilian Academy of Sciences 2010). At the time of writing (January 2013), a new code has been accepted by Congress, but the President Dilma Rouseff has vetoed parts of it, and its present status is uncertain.

The proposed new forest code constitutes an attempt to align Brazil's legal setting with, first, the actual situation on the ground – where, as we have seen, large-scale failures in terms of the stated objectives of the old code exist – and, second, with Brazilian interests in providing ever more land areas and land-based resources for the growing global socio-ecological metabolism. In this way, the new code should be seen as an adaptation by the Brazilian state to the global market's foreseeable future demand directed towards its rich land resources.

It was at first feared that the new code would lead to a reduction of the Legal Reserves by as much as 30 million hectares (or three times today's total sugar-cane land area), on account of a suggested diminuition of the Legal Reserves from 80 to 50 per cent of any holding in the Amazon (Sparovek *et al.* 2010a:8), but this proposal was later revoked. Still, the reserves will not be protected from "economic use" as long as it occurs "sustainably", and a similar opening is provided in relation to the Areas of Permanent Preservation.

Most contentious of all is that the proposed code offers a wholesale amnesty for all illegal land use which occurred before June 2008 (WWF Brasil 2011). This means that all breaches of the code which have been committed are retroactively pardoned, a severe strike against law-abiding property owners in the Amazon and elsewhere. As the code has been hotly debated in the Brazilian Congress, it is the retroactive approval of previous breaches of the code which has attracted the heaviest objections.

The officially embraced logic propelling the new code is that the protection of Brazilian lands has to be weakened in order to allow Brazilian agriculture to expand, but this has been questioned, as there already exist vast areas which could be used for agricultural purposes if only the area-efficiency of cattle raising was improved (Sparovek *et al.* 2010a, UNICA 2009; interviews with Gerd Sparovek and Donald Sawyer). Moreover, the statement by the Brazilian Academy of Sciences and the Brazilian Society for the Advancement of Science referred to above maintains that the new forest code "is based on the false premise that there is no land available for the expansion of Brazilian agriculture".

The freeing up of land by intensifying the use of pastures is similar to the highly controversial issue of using "degraded" and "abandoned" land for sugarcane. My interviewees responded to this proposition quite differently: from the very positive, "there are lots of degraded lands available, 60 million hectares, mostly pastures" (interview with Eduardo Assad), to the unambiguous refutation: such land areas do not exist. As one interviewee put it: "É pura mentira!" – it's a simple lie! (interview with Maria Luisa Mendonça).

## Sugarcane and land competition in Brazil

A central aspect when assessing the forest code relates to how one sees the process of expanding sugarcane cultivation. Is it a situation of peaceful coexistence among food, feed, fibre and fuel crops; or rather a conflictual process where different land uses collide with each other: new crops with old crops, old crops with old pastures, new pastures with forests?

Here, the very size of the Brazilian territory contributes to make little of the problem: although the land areas where expansion has taken place are large in absolute terms, they are quite small, almost insignificant, compared to the Brazilian territory as a whole. The Brazilian government takes advantage of this, using scale – the gigantic land areas supposedly available for use – as a pacifying response to all talk of conflicting land use. "No Brasil há muita terra" – Brazil has lots of land – was repeatedly the response I got when voicing concern over sugarcane expansion.

Take the increase of sugarcane cultivation which recently has occurred in Brazil: today the total land area of sugarcane – half for ethanol, half for sugar – is 8–9 million hectares, twice as much as only a decade ago. This has turned sugarcane cultivation into one of Brazil's most widely spread crops, superseded only by soybeans (which occupied 24 million hectares in 2010) and maize (13 million hectares in 2010; Conab 2010). As a consequence, sugar was Brazil's fourth most important export product in 2010 (after iron ore, oil and soybeans).

However, the Brazilian government can show that this is still a marginal share of Brazil's surface, only 1 per cent. Even if we consider doubling sugar production by 2017 – which is the government's plan – the new land areas will only require another 1 per cent of Brazil's territory. Table 3.1 shows how this is portrayed in the official presentation of the Brazilian "zoning" exercise to identify suitable land areas for sugarcane.

The actual competition of sugarcane → soybean → pastures → forests disappears amidst the overwhelming numbers. And should scale as such not be sufficiently reassuring, an authoritative state-of-the-art publication from the UN Food and Agriculture Organization, FAO, the UN Economic Commission for Latin America, ECLA, and the Brazilian state development bank, BNDES, assures us that the expansion of sugarcane "occurs on pastures" (BNDES and CGEE 2008:14). The statement is, as we will see, misleading, but it legitimizes the BNDES's support of sugarcane expansion and ethanol production through

*Table 3.1* Sugarcane cultivation and Brazil's land area, hectares and percentage of territory

| Land | Million hectares | Percentage of Brazil's territory |
|---|---|---|
| Total land area | 852 | 100 |
| Potential agricultural and pasture land | 554 | 65 |
| Agricultural land in use | 236 | 28 |
| Land areas suitable for sugarcane | 65 | 8 |
| Sugarcane land areas today | 8 | 1 |
| Sugarcane expansion until 2017 | 7 | 1 |

Source: Zoneamento Agroecológico de Cana-de-Açucar 2010.

the largest programme of its agro-industrial portfolio, close to six billion reais (US$3.5 billion) in 2009 (BNDES 2010).

The BNDES is important: were it to block access to finance, it would probably have a greater impact on sugarcane plantations and ethanol producers than codes and regulations as such. But BNDES is not known for being strict when it comes to abiding by rules, and it frequently disregards the misconduct of its partners in the Brazilian sugarcane-ethanol chain: out of 89 sugar plants which have obtained finance from the BNDES, only 15 have not been involved in labour, environmental or fiscal conflicts (Repórter Brasil 2011:14).

The up-beat conclusion about the non-competition between sugarcane and food has been used by UNICA to convince the EU and the US that Brazilian sugarcane ethanol will meet any environmental requirements which the importers may apply. In a letter to the European Commission, UNICA erroneously claims that the sugarcane zoning "forbids" sugarcane expansion in land areas rich in biodiversity (UNICA 2010). This is misleading for two reasons: first, the zoning is an indicative planning instrument with no legal power whatsoever; and, second, it does not rule out expansion in the Cerrado. The successful intention of UNICA was to ensure that the European Commission and the US Environmental Protection Agency included Brazilian sugarcane ethanol among the list of acceptable feedstocks to meet their respective mandatory blending requirements.

However, reality on the ground is very different from dreams of an ever-expanding agricultural frontier, where sugarcane never replaces existing crops. Studies of land-use change in the main sugarcane regions of Brazil show on the contrary that sugarcane expansion has replaced crops as well as pastures; most studies indicate that most of the land-use change occurs when sugarcane replaces pastures, but crop land is also targeted to a significant degree, going from 14 to 50 per cent of the area planted with sugarcane depending on the study (Aguiar *et al.* 2009, Neves do Amaral *et al.* 2008, Pires de Camargo 2008). The same holds for deforestation: although only limited areas are deforested to make room for sugarcane – assessments vary from 2 to as much as 15 per cent, the remainder being made up by pastures and crop lands – it does occur, and not infrequently.

As one of my interviewees said: "Temos prova da crime!" – we have evidence of the crime! (interview with Laerte Guimarães Ferreira).

But this is a snapshot – not an analysis of a process – and it disregards that the Cerrado had in many instances been cleared previously to make room for citrus and soybean. So the fact that only a minor share of the lands taken over by sugarcane were forested should not lead us to conclude that there is no land competition.

To understand the dynamics of land-use change we should realize that land is not acquired, and forests are not cut down, exclusively for agricultural or logging purposes. Land is transformed in a socio-economic process where speculation and money-laundering, drug trafficking and illicit mining, cattle raising and logging, all mix and blend with the expansion of agriculture and forestry for the production of food, feed, fibres and fuels (Hecht 2005:385–386; Sawyer 2008, 2009).

A landowner who sells a ranch in the southern and central parts of Brazil may use his money to acquire many times as large a holding in the north and north-east. In other words, land-use change is likely to have a multiplier effect: a small change on more expensive land will lead to larger changes on cheaper land.

For this reason, the attempt to belittle the competition over land by comparing the large land areas deforested in the Amazon with the comparatively small land areas dedicated to sugarcane is misleading. The underlying query is: how can large-scale deforestation in the Amazon be explained by small-scale sugarcane expansion? The study commissioned by the BNDES concludes that "the production of bioethanol does not imply deforestation" because the land area cleared in the Amazon from 1998 to 2007 was ten times larger than the area where sugarcane for fuel was introduced (BNDES and CGEE 2008:195). But this framing of the issue evades the more realistic assumption that when sugarcane replaces pastures, crops and Cerrado, more expensive land sold in the south of Brazil is turned into cheaper and larger land areas in the north.

Increasing land prices are relevant indicators of these processes, as the country as a whole constitutes one market when it comes to land. In the state of São Paulo, which is the main sugarcane region, land prices (in fixed terms) increased more than fourfold from 1999 to 2008 following the expansion of sugarcane cultivation in that state (Novo *et al.* 2010:783).

Normally, before land-use change takes place, the ownership of land has changed hands. In the Amazon, the land may go back and forth between owners, implying concomitantly a series of land-use changes:

> The land in a particular place may start as public land and be invaded either by large "grileiros" [landgrabbers], by individual squatters, or by "sem terras" [landless]. Ranchers may purchase large blocks of land from "grileiros" or may buy a number of small colonist lots. The ranches can be invaded by squatters or "sem terras", or, if the land is economically attractive for soybeans, the properties can be sold to capitalized farmers.
>
> (Fearnside 2008)

This land-use change process does not stop at national borders: as land areas are taken over from pastures or food crops by sugarcane and soybeans, land acquisition outside of Brazil also follows. One indication of this is the growing presence of Brazilian commercial farming capital in Bolivia (Hecht 2005). Here, as in the expansion of sugarcane cultivation in general, there are various actors engaged, from state banks which provide finance, to public agricultural research agencies which promote high-yielding seeds (Mackey 2011).

The list of international corporations and joint ventures involved is impressive: large transnational corporations in the energy and agro-business field – from Dreyfus and Cargill to Dow and Shell – are competing for Brazilian land resources with countries such as China and India, sometimes in joint ventures, for instance between Japan and Brazil, represented by the state oil giant Petrobras (Wilkinson and Herrera 2010:751–752; Repórter Brasil 2010:58–59).

There is also a domestic component to this international effect. The Brazilian state subsidizes the expansion of commercial crops – primarily soybeans and sugarcane – and simultaneously opens the door for international agrocorporations. This support includes cheap credits; the construction of infrastructure, especially roads and railroads, which open up new land areas for commercial agriculture; and connecting the major production regions with the coast via two ethanol pipelines, called *alcooldutos*, running from the interior sugarcane and ethanol zones of Brazil to the coast (Pietrafesa *et al.* 2009). Today, after spending public funds "for decades", the Brazilian state is offering domestic and foreign investors land that it can portray as "ready, productive and technologically efficient" (Pietrafesa *et al.* 2010:14).

## Taking carbon emissions and biodiversity into account

The Brazilian laws and regulations relating to land use must be seen in their international context: since Brazil aims to sell agrofuel on the global market, it will be subject to the laws, regulations and certification schemes which are being established at the user end, most importantly by the US and the EU. For these schemes, the impact of agrofuel feedstocks on biodiversity and carbon emissions is a key concern.

Initially, the impact of agrofuels was assessed by applying life cycle analyses, LCAs, in order to capture the environmental impact of the production and combustion of agrofuels from field to exhaust pipe; the results were quite encouraging, and agrofuels were held to be "climate neutral". But this outcome was to a large extent due to the fact that LCAs do not as a rule take all relevant factors into consideration. Although early LCAs did include indirect use of fossil fuels – fertilizers and other fossil-based inputs, as well as fuels spent in production and transportation – they customarily disregarded the effects of direct land-use change on the release of greenhouse gases (GHG).

Bringing direct land-use change into the picture significantly alters the performance of the feedstocks concerned. In Table 3.2, the number of years before agrofuels have paid back their carbon debt is shown depending on the previous land use. With the exception of degraded lands, the number of years before GHG neutrality will be achieved is surprisingly high, except for Brazilian sugarcane (where the case of sugarcane in Cerrado is an exception; as we have seen, most sugarcane ethanol in Brazil has expanded on crop lands and pastures, and hence the pay-back period is still considerably shorter).

For the remaining feedstocks, the time periods needed to make up for the greenhouse gases emitted when clearing grasslands and forests are much, and sometimes very much, longer. The worst case is transforming rainforest peatland to palm oil, with a repayment period of 423 years. This may seem like an extreme value, but another assessment of palm oil on peatland by the Intergovernmental Panel on Climate Change (IPCC) concluded that the pay-back period until carbon neutrality could be as high as 900 years (IPCC 2011, Figure 2:12).

However, great uncertainty still reigns concerning the carbon pay-back periods when the feedstocks take over already cropped lands. An IPCC-sponsored state-of-the art study on renewable energies concluded – contrary to Table 3.2 – that pay-back was more or less immediate when crop land was transferred to cater to agrofuels; on the other hand, the conclusion regarding converting forests (not to speak of peatlands) into agrofuels was conclusively negative: "all biofuel options have significant payback times when dense forests are converted into bioenergy plantations" (IPCC 2011:2:77). But *direct* land-use change is only the first step in assessing the impact from expanding agrofuel feedstocks; *indirect* effects should also be considered, if possible. In Brazil the sequence of land-use change has often been, taking São Paulo as an example: Cerrado → citrus, citrus → soybean, soybean → sugarcane; at the same time pasture → soybean and sugarcane, and forests and Cerrado → pasture, either in close proximity to the expanding agricultural areas – that is in the Cerrado – or further away, for instance in the Amazon.

*Table 3.2* Feedstock performance with direct land-use change included

| Feedstock/fuel | Original land use | Location | Years to recover $CO_2$ |
|---|---|---|---|
| Prairie biomass/ethanol | Marginal crop land | USA | 0 |
| Prairie biomass/ethanol | Abandoned crop land | USA | 1 |
| Sugarcane/ethanol | Cerrado wooded | Brazil | 17 |
| Soybean/biodiesel | Cerrado grassland | Brazil | 37 |
| Maize/ethanol | Abandoned crop land | USA | 48 |
| Palm oil/biodiesel | Tropical rainforest | Indonesia, Malaysia | 86 |
| Maize/ethanol | Central grassland | USA | 93 |
| Soybean/biodiesel | Tropical rainforest | Brazil | 319 |
| Palm oil/biodiesel | Peatland rainforest | Indonesia, Malaysia | 423 |

Source: Fargione *et al.* 2008, Figure 1.

Note
Indirect land-use change not included.

This is not the way that the sugarcane and ethanol industry would like us to think about the potential land conflicts in Brazil; rather it prefers to give the impression that sugarcane expansion has nothing to do with what happens in other parts of Brazil. UNICA is fond of showing a map – for instance to Maud Olofsson, then Swedish minister for enterprise, when she visited Brazil in 2008 – which conveys the impression that as the sugarcane zones in the southeast and northeast of the country are 2,000–2,500 km removed from the sensitive Amazon biome (not the Legal Amazon), and that there is hence no reason for a prospective importer such as Sweden to waver: there is no reason to fear that expansion of the production of sugarcane ethanol would affect the Amazon negatively. The trick is performed by UNICA to this very day (UNICA 2011a:16).

Brazilian sugarcane is indeed grown far away from the Amazon, but the presentation is nevertheless misleading, in three respects. First, the major sugarcane zones have biodiversity problems of their own, of no less consequence than those in the Amazon, as we have seen; and planting sugarcane (or any other crop) on Cerrado lands may be as dubious an activity as planting it in the Amazon, from an ecological point of view. Put differently, the UNICA pretends that there is no *direct* land-use change issue in relation to the expansion of sugarcane cultivation.

Second, the way UNICA frames the issue dodges the whole issue of *indirect* land-use change; they simply show no knock-on effects from scaling up sugarcane plantations.

And third, the illusion of small numbers is taken advantage of: with only 1–2 per cent of Brazil's arable land set aside for sugarcane – see Table 3.1 above – why should a Swedish minister worry?

It must be recognized, however, that accounting for indirect effects is not easy to do reliably; it adds insecurity to the assessments, as the links and impacts are difficult to model. While direct land-use change can be measured with satellite images or on the ground, indirect land-use change is a modelling exercise. The most influential study on *indirect* land-use change to date (Searchinger *et al.* 2008) models the impact of increasing US maize ethanol production on land use in Brazil, China, India and the US itself, and concludes that the pay-back time for US maize to reach climate neutrality would be 167 years, considerably longer than with direct land-use change only, as shown in Table 3.2 above, where it was 93 years.

The European Commission recently concluded that there is significant insecurity in the estimates of indirect land-use change as a consequence of the EU's mandate of 10 per cent renewable fuels in the transport sector by 2020, as stated in its Renewable Energy Directive (RED, European Union 2009). In one simulation, one million hectares of indirect land-use change took place; in another, five million hectares, approximately equal to the whole sugarcane land area set aside for ethanol in Brazil. The gap between the lowest and the highest for indirect land-use change was seven times for maize ethanol, and five times for soybean biodiesel (European Commission 2010). In other words, there is no generally accepted methodology for measuring indirect land-use change.

A common conclusion of the studies of agrofuels and land-use change, direct and indirect, is that the assessments vary. The underlying assumptions decide the result: what feedstock on what land replaces what previous land use, and results in what knock-on impact when the ousted land use moves to new lands? The only commonly agreed position, so far, is that land-use change caused by expanding agrofuels will result in net negative emissions for considerable periods of time, extending at least over a couple of decades; this holds for all feedstocks, including sugarcane, and for all previous land uses (except abandoned crop lands; Berndes *et al.* 2010:13 and Figure 9).

The conclusion is that with today's technique and feedstocks, agrofuels' ecological credentials are not convincing. In fact, including direct and indirect land-use change makes defending agrofuels with ecological arguments next to impossible: the time horizon is simply pushed too far into the future to be meaningful for a policy that attempts to contribute to stabilizing the climate in the short to medium term.

Furthermore, climate stability is not the only ecological issue to be concerned about when it comes to agrofuels; their impact on biodiversity has also become an issue, as shown in Table 3.3. There should be no doubt that monocultures of the kind we witness in the production of agrofuel feedstocks are antithetical to high levels of biodiversity, and transforming diverse crop lands to sugarcane or maize plantations will lead to serious reductions in biodiversity (Dale *et al.* 2010:4–5).

A positive biodiversity effect is expected in the short run *only* if agrofuel feedstocks are planted on abandoned and previously intensively cultivated lands; for all other land-use changes, the production of agrofuel feedstocks will lead to biodiversity loss for at least 100 years.

*Table 3.3* Biodiversity impact of land-use change

| Land cover converted to agrofuel feedstock | Positive impact on biodiversity | Negative impact on biodiversity |
|---|---|---|
| Recently abandoned land after intensive use | Immediately positive but not substantial until after 100 years, <+25% | – |
| Recently abandoned land after extensive use | Mildly positive after 100 years, <+25% | Immediately negative, <–25% |
| Abandoned partly restored lands | – | Immediately negative, >–25%; after 100 years still –10 to –25% |
| Grasslands extensively used | – | Immediately negative, >–50%; after 100 years still –25% |
| Natural grasslands and forests | – | Immediately negative, >–75%; after 100 years still –60% |

Source: UNEP 2009:71.

Note
Impact on biodiversity is measured in terms of percentage change of mean species abundance.

Here we can detect a dilemma for the proponents of agrofuels in climate policy: while climate change impacts biodiversity negatively, so does growing feedstocks for agrofuels. Even if you believe that agrofuels are "climate neutral" – a doubtful assumption, as we have seen – their negative impact on biodiversity may be greater than the positive effect reaped from reducing GHG. The balance of these two counter-movements, according to the only assessment which I have come across, is not favourable, and the authors reach this conclusion without even considering the soil carbon emissions which are caused by land-use change:

> An analysis with a "biodiversity balance" indicator shows that the green-house gas reductions from biofuel production are insufficient to compensate for biodiversity losses from land use change, in most cases. This result will be even worse when soil carbon emissions from land use change are taken into account.
>
> (Eickhout *et al.* 2008:48)

As we saw in Table 3.3, the environmentally most advantageous conversion to agrofuel feedstocks takes place on land that already has been cleared but which now is abandoned. However, the assumption that there are "unused" land areas available for agrofuel production has been questioned: apart from the fact that land classified as "marginal" and "abandoned" is often used land and not vacant (fallow lands, for instance), such lands may also be rich in biodiversity and are not empty of species (IPCC 2011:2:30). Hence, even the planting of agrofuel feedstocks on "marginal" lands – should they exist – in order to undo their negative carbon balance may in fact damage important ecosystem services: "The transformation of M[arginal] L[ands] for biofuel production may yield a lasting legacy of environmental disruption" (Gutierrez and Ponti 2009:221).

## Certification schemes and mandatory regulation

As I noted in the previous chapter, large-scale ethanol production did not originate as a tool of climate policy, but has been fomented for geopolitical reasons, first in Brazil following the oil price hikes of 1973–1974, and then more recently in the US and the EU to reduce the dependence on oil. Today, this objective is supported by claims that agrofuels may slow down climate change, thus "green-washing" the mandatory blending requirements which have been introduced in recent years.

Transferring the direct and indirect impacts of the expansion of sugarcane cultivation into regulations and certification schemes is no easy matter. The literature abounds with statements stressing the complexity of the task, and in a survey of the issues that need to be tackled in order to make certification of agrofuels "work for sustainable development", the UN Conference on Trade and Development (UNCTAD) concluded that there are 127 concerns which have to be accounted for, 47 of which deal with ecological issues (UNCTAD 2008:45–48).

If one difficulty here is the sheer number of aspects that a certification scheme has to address in order to capture social and ecological sustainability, another is the abundance of certification schemes that are being promoted. In one count, UNICA found over 30 schemes and regulatory frameworks throughout the world; every major actor is establishing its own rules for what constitutes acceptable agrofuels. This surge in certification schemes, and the various demands and requirements directed from different markets, have met with resistance from the agrofuel industry, and UNICA talks of a "'universe' in constant expansion" (UNICA 2011b:67).

A spokesperson of the agrofuel industry laments that the many certification schemes slow down the turning of ethanol and biodiesel into commodities to be traded on an international exchange, as oil is. In the port of Santos, the ethanol industry complains, ethanol has to be stored separately depending on the market, one tank for Sweden, another for France; and this separation holds also when ethanol is loaded on to the exporting ships, as if the liquids were qualitatively different just because they have to conform to different certification schemes (Bioenergia 2009).

To gain credibility, most of these certification schemes involve a large number of actors in the elaboration of criteria and principles, mixing energy corporations, environmental non-governmental organizations (NGOs), states, and national and international financial institutions. Consider, for instance, the Roundtable on Sustainable Biofuels, RSB, one of the most influential attempts to establish globally accepted criteria for certification (RSB 2012). The RSB brings together environmental organizations (such as the World Wildlife Fund and the International Union for Conservation of Nature, both initiators of the RSB), big corporations (Petrobras, Boeing, Shell), banks (Inter-American Development Bank), ethanol producers (UNICA), rural development NGOs, UN organizations (UNEP, UNCTAD) and governments (Switzerland). After spending years deliberating, the RSB proposed 12 principles for "sustainable biofuels", covering issues ranging from land rights to greenhouse gas emissions. However, meeting the RSB's standards does not mean that the fuel in question is acceptable from an ecological point of view. Surprisingly, the RSB, in spite of its name, does not take a stand on the sustainability of the fuels it certifies: "the Principles and Criteria do not attempt to quantify an amount of biofuels which could be sustainably produced, *or whether, as a whole, biofuels are sustainable*" (RSB 2010:3, italics added). My understanding of such certification schemes is that they do not contribute to changing the way agrofuels are being produced *unless they establish what they will not accept*: which feedstocks are unacceptable, and where acceptable feedstocks cannot be grown. Such schemes have a potential of actually directing agrofuel development in conformity with declared principles, be they social or ecological.

The US and the EU have chosen different approaches here. The US Environmental Protection Agency has "determined" that ethanol produced from maize saves 20 per cent of greenhouse gases, just as it has "determined" that sugarcane ethanol saves 50 per cent, which qualify them for fulfilling the targets established by the US Energy Independence and Security Act (EPA 2010:5). This decision prompted 190 scientists to warn the US Congress that standards and benchmarks for agrofuels that are to contribute to climate stability have to be carefully thought through: "The lesson is that any legal measure to reduce greenhouse gas emissions must include a system to differentiate emissions from bioenergy based on the source of the biomass" (Open Letter 2010).

The wholesale acceptance of questionable feedstocks reinforces the already strong likelihood that the US mandate – 137 billion litres by 2022 – will stimulate increased production of feedstocks not only in the US but equally abroad, and thus cause direct land-use change domestically as well as globally, and on a large scale considering the large volumes mandated. However, going one step further by adding indirect land-use change, as we should in order to correctly assess the whole impact of expanding agrofuels, is perhaps asking too much of the regulation, since any such calculation would have to be based on hypotheses regarding land-use patterns globally.

The EU RED of 2009 is also part of this trend – mandating 10 per cent renewable energy in transport by 2020, most of it agrofuels – but it appears to be more restrictive in accepting feedstocks to meet its objective: no feedstocks grown on "land with high biodiversity value", or on lands with high carbon stocks, will be accepted. The types of land area which are off limits are specified in the RED (European Union 2009, Article 17:3–5). Agrofuels should not be grown on:

- primary forests and other wooded lands;
- land areas set aside for nature protection and for the protection of rare, threatened and endangered ecosystems;
- highly biodiverse grasslands;
- wetlands and continuously forested land areas with trees higher than five metres and a canopy of more than 30 per cent;
- peatland.

This would arguably make it quite difficult to find suitable new land areas to meet the EU blending requirement. For instance, Brazil's Cerrado, with its high biodiversity value, would not be permissible for agrofuel expansion if Brazil wants to adhere to EU requirements. And biodiesel from Indonesian and Malaysian palm oil plantations in the rainforest would equally be unacceptable.

Without negative screening, certification schemes will tend to "green-wash" rather than provide reliable and verifiable rules for the sustainable production of agrofuels. One reason has to do with the aggregation of criteria and conditions: how do you assess an agrofuel when some factors are acceptable and some are not? For instance, a Dutch survey of 17 social and environmental criteria for judging Brazilian ethanol held that "only" two criteria were problematic: biodiversity and competition with food production. Is this to be viewed as a serious limitation of Brazilian sugarcane ethanol, or should this fuel be accepted based on the fact that most of the criteria were met? The study bravely concluded, in spite of the recognized drawbacks, that there were "no prohibitive reasons ...

identified why ethanol from São Paulo principally could not meet the Dutch sustainability standards" (Smeets *et al.* 2006:2). Another problem with the certification approach is that some principles have almost zero possibility of being met if you take them at face value. Is it a realistic requirement that agrofuels should avoid impacting negatively on biodiversity, as stipulated by Principle 7 of the RSB? It is, as we have seen, unlikely that any of today's feedstocks would pass this test.

To the delineation of which lands may and which may not be used for agrofuels feedstocks, we must add the differences among the various feedstocks: they are not equally good or bad. One list of preferred feedstocks – called "biofuels done right" – only accepts five feedstocks in order not to compete with food, damage biodiversity, or contribute to greenhouse gas emissions (Tilman *et al.* 2009):

*   perennial plants on degraded lands;
*   crop residues;
*   wood and forest residues;
*   double crops and mixed cropping systems;
*   municipal and industrial wastes.

The list is almost identical to the one published by the International Energy Agency in its *Technology Roadmap: Biofuels for Transport*, where only the following feedstocks are allowed in order to minimize "the risks of land use change and resulting emissions": wastes and residues, perennial energy corps on unproductive or low-carbon soils, and co-production of energy and food crops (IEA 2011b:18). With such a limited list of acceptable feedstocks, one would be excused for thinking that the International Energy Agency (IEA) – an organ of the Organization for Economic Cooperation and Development (OECD) – sees a continuation of the present fossil-nuclear metabolic regime rather than its replacement by agrofuels.

Most remarkable in these attempts to find acceptable feedstocks is that none of today's favoured crops – sugarcane and maize for ethanol, and rape seed, soybeans and palm oil for biodiesel – will qualify (unless they are part of mixed or double cropping systems which tend to rule out large-scale plantations and mechanization). In fact the lists could be read as a serious objection to the way agrofuels are developed under present conditions, following pathways with "several wrong options" (Tilman *et al.* 2009:271), which means that the risk that agrofuels will increase greenhouse gas emissions, endanger biodiversity, and push out food production is imminent and should be the overriding concern. Put differently, agrofuels today are certainly done the wrong way.

This conclusion may appear too strong, but it was recently corroborated by a surprising proposal tabled by the European Commission to limit the use of agrofuels in fulfilment of the EU 2009 RED. Recognizing the competition for land, the Commission now proposes that no agricultural feedstocks in addition to the 5 per cent currently mandated in the EU should be introduced, as they cannot help but compete with food (European Commission 2012).

This is a considerable setback for the agrofuel lobby worldwide, and it is not certain that the proposal will be accepted. But it testifies to the growing realization, in some unexpected quarters, of the significance of direct and indirect land-use change to the ecological credentials of agrofuels.

## Concluding remarks

The pressure on Brazilian land areas for sugarcane and other essential feedstocks (such as soybean for biodiesel, and eucalyptus for paper) is part of a new scramble for land areas. Such pressures have a tendency to permeate the global agricultural system, erasing the border that distinguishes domestic from international, and international from global. As we have seen, Elinor Ostrom realized that in situations like this, with the land-use impacts felt over large distances and across borders, small self-regulating governance systems are of no guidance.

The national codes and agreements which regulate Brazil's sugarcane industry (for instance the forest code, the zoning plan, the voluntary agreement on working conditions) are essential, but they are only partly successful in terms of their actual implementation on the ground. However, they could also be interpreted as a success in that they have convinced the US and the EU that Brazilian ethanol is pure, clean and no threat to biodiversity.

Although environmental concerns may not constitute the main driver here, they nevertheless provide the ecological stamp of approval that is needed. As a consequence, agrofuels, in spite of all of their drawbacks, are poised to go on expanding, especially with the steps already taken by states around the world to increase the share of agrofuels in their respective energy mixes (see Table 2.2 above).

In this perspective, certification schemes, in order to impact actual land use and land-use change, must focus on combining a short list of acceptable feedstocks with an equally restricted list of land areas where they can be grown: not very encouraging for the geopolitically driven attempt of finding an alternative to fossil fuels in the short and medium term.

As we have seen, it is possible to imagine a totally different pathway for the future of agrofuels in countries with a large potential for producing feedstocks such as Brazil: by intensifying cattle grazing, pastures could be freed for agrofuels, which would permit a multiplication of sugarcane areas without entering into an immediate conflict with other lands for food, feed and fibres.

However, even if an intensification of cattle-ranching –zero-grazing was even suggested to me as an option by some of my interviewees – would free land for sugarcane and soybean without *forcing* ranchers to look for new pastures, it is likely that they would do so anyway, since their lands would gain in value when agrofuel feedstocks expand. Thus, the further spread of agrofuel would still set a process of indirect land-use change in motion, leading to the conclusion that agrofuels are not the answer to the search for environmentally friendly energy carriers.

On the other hand, if it is geopolitics and not environmental preoccupations which are at the forefront of the drive to promote agrofuels, the ecological drawbacks will not constitute a decisive blockage to their continued expansion.

## Interviewees

Assad, Eduardo: Senior Researcher, Embrapa, Campinas

Assad de Ávila, Silvia: Researcher, Centre for Sustainable Development, Universidade de Brasília, Brasília

Ávila, Mário: Researcher, Centre for Sustainable Development, Universidade de Brasília, Brasília

Canuto, Antônio: Coordinator, Comissão dos Pastores da Terra, Goiânia

Ferreira, Laerte Guimarães: Coordinator, Laboratório de Processamento de Imagens e Geoprocessamento, Universidade Federal de Goiás, Goiânia

Garrido, Valdemar: President, Sindicatos dos Trabalhadores e Trabalhadoras Rurais de Indiara, Goiás

Mendonça, Maria Luisa: Executive Director, Rede Social de Justiça e Direitos Humanos, São Paulo

de Moura, Fábio Alves: Agricultural Supervisor, Denusa Sugar Mill, Indiara, Goiás

Panceroli, Paulo: cane cutter, Ester Sugar Plant, Cosmópolis

Pietrafesa, José Paulo: Research Coordinator, UniEvangélica, Anápolis

Sawyer, Donald: Advisor, Instituto Sociedade, População e Natureza, and Vice-Director, Centre for Sustainable Development, Universidade de Brasília, Brasília

Silva, Maria Aparecida de Moraes: Professor, Universidade Estadual Paulista and Universidade Federal de São Carlos, São Carlos

Sparovek, Gerd: Professor, Luiz de Queiroz College of Agriculture, Universidade de São Paulo, Piracicaba

Widriweski, Isolete: Coordinator, Comissão dos pastores da terra, Goiânia

# Part II

# Ecologically unequal exchange

I have argued that land areas and land-based resources will become of ever greater importance to the global socio-ecological metabolic regime. This implies that the access to, and the control over, such resources will be of central concern to the dominating economic powers.

In this part of the book, I want to investigate whether the centrality of land areas and land-based resources is reflected in the way that economies trade with each other, in their actual trading patterns: do rich and powerful economies appropriate land areas from poor economies? How can this exchange be measured?

To be able to say something meaningful about unequal exchange, I need to divide the economies of the world into different categories, which is no clean-cut matter. The terms Centre/Periphery, rich/poor, developed/developing, North/South, high-income/low-income all carry two drawbacks. First, they entail a sense of historic progress, a certain Eurocentrism, where Centre and North transmit a connotation of "developed" and "better", in one word, "modern". Second, the dichotomization does not reflect reality well; economies end up as special cases, occupying in-between categories such as semi-centre, semi-periphery, or middle-income.

I prefer the terms coined by the global justice movement, global North and global South, indicating that there are rich people in poor countries just as there are poor people in rich ones. But going down this road would lead me to another blockage, the fact that trade statistics is based on states, which forces me to rely on data for "the amorphous blurs known as national economies", to use urban historian Jane Jacob's apt phrase (Jacobs 1985:44).

In the following chapters I am restricted to the classifications applied by other researchers, and they typically use income-based categories, which I must in those cases also make do with. Furthermore, when it comes to energy statistics, the best available information is often provided by the International Energy Agency (IEA) – an institution of the Organization for Economic Cooperation and Development (OECD) – which uses OECD and non-OECD membership to classify countries, something I also will do occasionally. In addition, most of the measures of embodied carbon relate to the UN Framework Convention on Climate Change and use its listing (Annex I and Non-Annex I countries) or follow its Kyoto protocol (Annex B and Non-Annex B countries) to distinguish countries with and without obligations to reduce $CO_2$ emissions.

In this confusing multitude of delimitations I have opted for an ecumenical stance and will use the concepts freely and interchangeably, more or less following the categories applied by the sources on which I rely. Thus when I discuss the theory of deteriorating terms-of-trade for raw materials, it is appropriate to use Centre/Periphery, since this is the context where this dichotomy was first introduced.

# 4 Framing unequal exchange

That international exchange may be biased in favour of some traders at the expense of others is not a new insight, but rather as old as trade theory itself: exchange among economies which are different – different climates, different endowments with productive resources such as land, labour and capital – means that one trading partner benefits more than the other. In this sense, all trade is unequal, and Paul Krugman even calls unequal exchange "inevitable" in his influential textbook *International Economics*: "It is clear that the trade between advanced countries and developing countries is marked by 'unequal exchange'" (Krugman and Obstfeld 1994:269). But Krugman does not conclude from this clear-sightedness that poor countries should attempt to become more self-sustained or inward-looking in their development strategies. No: the correct comparison, he claims, is not between importing and exporting economies, but rather with what "it would have taken to produce your imports yourself" (Krugman and Obstfeld 1994:22). If a poor economy has to expend more resources to produce a certain good, it had better import it from an economy which can produce it with fewer. The fact that the poor economy is exchanging more land, labour, or capital for less is of no concern. In other words, this kind of trade theory is more interested in the allocation of a certain volume of production than with the development trajectory of poor economies.

For the study of unequal exchange, the focus is on the trajectory of economies as well as on the disparities between them. Historically, the framing of unequal exchange has taken place along two parallel logics, one related to labour and one related to energy. The real significance of exchange, it is held in both of these traditions, cannot be measured by the monetary value of the exchanged goods, but will only be grasped by measuring the exchange in another metric: embodied labour hours in the Marxist economics tradition, most famously expounded by economist Arghiri Emmanuel (1972); embodied energy in the ecological tradition, where Howard Odum's is the key contribution (1996).

The two approaches are similar in that both argue from the point of view of a theory of value – that is, they each claim that the real value of the goods exchanged is different from what the monetary value discloses, and that embodied labour or embodied energy, respectively, is to be preferred to other measures in order to unveil what really is going on under the guise of equal monetary exchange. In this sense these traditions mirror each other in their attempt to capture "the appropriate measure of value", be it labour or energy (Lonergan 1988:130 and 133–134).

My interest in discussing unequal exchange is not to assess the "real value" of the exchange, however, but rather to measure exchange in a non-monetary metric which serves my focus on land areas and land-based resources, leading me to prefer measures of embodied exchange of biophysical resources. From the point of view of the history of the concept of unequal exchange, however, the focus is on the purchasing power of different commodities. After World War II, a straightforward argument was made advising poor economies that export raw materials to avoid the trap of engaging in an international division of labour which placed them at a disadvantage. Simply to go along with traditional theories would be ill advised, the Argentinian economist Raúl Prebisch wrote in 1950. The "outdated schema of international division of labour" carried "a flaw" in recommending the same policies to poor and rich countries: "The enormous benefits that derive from the increased productivity have not reached the periphery in a measure comparable to that obtained by the peoples of the great industrial countries" (Prebisch 1950:1).

Prebisch claimed that the positive attitude to exposing your economy to international competition rested on committing the error of "generalizing from the particular". The already industrial countries constituted a particular case, according to Prebisch; suggesting that today's Periphery should do as today's Centre did was "based upon an assumption which has been conclusively proved false by facts", namely that "the benefits of technical progress tend to be distributed alike over the whole community" and that hence the "countries producing raw materials obtain their share of these benefits through international exchange, and therefore have no need to industrialize" (Prebisch 1950:1).

The "assumption" that Prebisch inveighed against – that trade benefits all parties – goes back to classical economist David Ricardo, who, 133 years prior to Prebisch, argued in favour of opening up countries to international competition. Ricardo presented a new argument for exposing a national market to foreign competitors, and one which played into the hands of his native country, Great Britain, the dominant industrial power at the time. As we saw in Chapter 1, Britain's socio-ecological metabolic regime had already become dependent on importing embodied land areas and land-based resources in great quantities; now it also needed to find markets for its industrial produce.

Ricardo's position was based on a model economy which assumed that capital could not cross borders. This is the most essential pre-condition for Ricardo's argument, as otherwise – "if capital freely flowed to those countries where it could be most profitably employed", as Ricardo himself wrote – there would be no difference in prices between different countries, and hence no reason to trade (Ricardo 2006/1817:95). As a consequence, everyone would suffer, Ricardo claimed: the seller from being restricted to a smaller market, the buyer by having access to fewer goods at higher prices.

Ricardo also stressed another benefit of trade which came to the fore much later: the peace argument. He framed this with the same logic that Adam Smith used when he argued for the existence of a market mechanism which like an "invisible hand" turned individuals' self-serving behaviour into a common good:

> Under a system of perfectly free commerce, each country naturally devotes its capital and labour to such employments as are most beneficial to each. This pursuit of individual advantage is admirably connected with the universal good of the whole.... while by increasing the general mass of productions, it diffuses general benefit, and binds together, by one common tie of interest and intercourse, the universal society of nations throughout the civilized world. It is this principle which determines that wine shall be made in France and Portugal, that corn shall be grown in America and Poland, and that hardware and other goods shall be manufactured in England.
>
> (Ricardo 2006/1817:93)

Neither the Rome Charter of 1957, the founding document of today's European Union, nor the preamble of the statutes of the World Trade Organization from 1995, has put the pacifying impact of international trade in more alluring terms. But note that the only producer of manufactures mentioned by Ricardo was England.

According to Ricardo, all countries ought to open up to trade, to the benefit of all. Even countries that had no advantages in terms of productivity, climate, resources or knowledge were well advised to specialize and trade with their superior competitors, as this would increase the overall welfare of both the trading countries. In words that have entered standard economics textbooks, a country should exploit its *comparative* advantages – even if all of them were *absolute* disadvantages.

This was not so, however, according to Prebisch: "outward-oriented development" was "incapable of permitting the full development of [Latin American] countries" (Prebisch 1984:177). As a result, a more inward-oriented policy proposed itself.

Prebisch based his argument on a study of declining raw materials prices by economist Hans Singer, who showed that the purchasing power of primary commodities had declined by 31 per cent from 1876 to 1947 (Singer 1950). Singer says that he was led in this direction by his teacher in Cambridge from 1934 to 1936, the economist John Maynard Keynes, who shared the idea "that primary commodity prices would have a long-run downward trend" (Singer 1984:279). Singer's friendly reference to Keynes for inspiration may owe something to the fact that Keynes "tirelessly" (and successfully) petitioned to have Singer released from his internment by the British authorities as an "enemy alien" after his escape from the Nazis (Skidelsky 2000:78). Keynes wrote to a friend in his typical style in July 1940, two years before Stalingrad and while the Battle of Britain was still raging:

Our behaviour towards refugees is the most disgraceful and humiliating thing which has happened for a long time. Also rather disconcerting to find that we have such obvious fatheads still in charge ... if there are any Nazi sympathisers still at large in this country, we should look in the War Office and our Secret Service, not in the internment camps.

(quoted in Harrod 1963:497)

Singer explained the falling tendency of raw materials' prices in relation to their low sensitivity to price and income: when prices fall or incomes grow, the demand for food and other primary commodities increases, but not very much. In the case of manufactures, however, the situation is the opposite: the demand for industrial goods grows faster than income. In economists' parlance: raw materials have low (<1) and industrial goods high (>1) price and income elasticity. In addition, Singer stipulates a general trend of increasing efficiency, whereby technical progress leads to "a reduction in the amount of raw materials used per unit of output, which may compensate or even overcompensate the increase in the volume of manufacturing output" (Singer 1950:479). In other words, a country which tries to develop by increasing its exports of primary commodities will be confronted by reduced purchasing power in terms of the industrial goods that it can acquire. This, then, is the Prebisch–Singer hypothesis, PSH, in short: specialization and division of labour along the raw materials/industrial goods axis will lead to unequal development.

## Testing the Prebisch–Singer hypothesis

Prebisch and Singer's warning, that trade can constrain countries by keeping them poor and dependent on raw materials, has sounded repeatedly in the development discourse – although not in the mainstream economics textbooks – for 60 years. From the unequal development of purchasing power it follows that trade may lead to a transfer of resources, and that international exchange thus may constitute a process which amasses riches and power in certain parts of the global system, while simultaneously creating poverty and powerlessness elsewhere.

The real test of the Prebisch–Singer Hypothesis is not theoretical, however, but empirical. Singer himself updated his analysis repeatedly, and at the same time broadened the approach by adding to his original argument – focused on raw materials exports – the position of the countries in the global hierarchy. While relying on exporting primary products cannot be recommended – he noted a decline of terms-of-trade by more than 2 per cent per annum from 1972 to 1986 – exporting manufactures from the Periphery is almost equally negative, as exports of industrial goods from the Periphery also suffer a gradual erosion of purchasing power measured in relation to its imports of manufactures from the Centre, minus 1 per cent per year from 1970 to 1987 (Sarkar and Singer 1991:338). Thus, the Periphery comes out poorly irrespective of what it exports: primary commodities are bad, and manufactures are not good.

What Singer is doing here is in fact combining two approaches – terms-of-trade decline as a consequence of the products traded, and as a consequence of the hierarchical position in the economy – into one argument. He thereby confirms both what is called the PSH I (considering the nature of primary commodities, frequently attributed to Singer), and the PSH II (considering the position of countries in the Centre versus the Periphery, Prebisch's focus in his 1950 study; see Ocampo and Parra 2003:8).

That raw materials indeed have lost purchasing power during the last century is graphically shown in Figure 4.1. However, there has not been a smooth and continuous downward trend, but rather four dramatic shifts of the terms-of-trade of primary commodities, first upwards, then abruptly and even more steeply downwards, first boom, then bust: World War I, World War II, the mid-1970s initiated by the rise in oil prices, and then again during the present phase which began in the early 2000s and collapsed, temporarily, as we have seen, in 2008.

Is this downward movement of the terms-of-trade of raw materials of any importance to poor countries? Yes, the cumulative loss of purchasing power of primary commodities (based on 24 raw materials but excluding oil, a standard procedure) amounted to as much as two-thirds from 1900 to 2000, not an inconsequential deterioration (Ocampo and Parra 2003; Zania 2005).

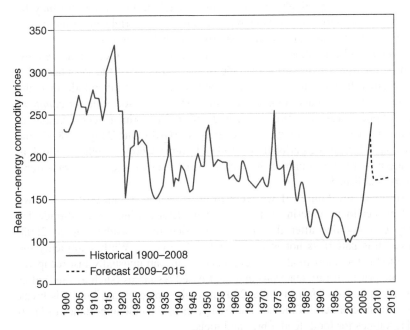

*Figure 4.1* Historical terms-of-trade, 1900–2008, with a forecast to 2015; indexes, 2000=0, deflated by unit value of manufactured exports; the forecast – the dashed line – has not been borne out so far (source: Brahmbhatt and Canuto 2010, © World Bank, Washington, DC; License: CC BY 3.0; unported, used with permisson).

The evidence is thus strong for the validity of the PSH in spite of continuous attempts to refute it (see for instance Kellard and Wohar 2006). What is more, the PSH also seems to be valid for an even longer historic period, at least if we are to believe the only really long-term study that I have come across, spanning three centuries. Of the 25 major commodities that are included here – with varying longitudinal data, some series beginning as early as 1650, some as late as 1900 – almost half have shown consistently deteriorating terms-of-trade: aluminium, coffee, hides, jute, silver, sugar, tobacco, tea, wheat, wool and zinc. For instance, coffee has lost an average of 0.77 per cent of purchasing power annually for 300 years. The remaining commodities – bananas, beef, coal, cocoa, copper, cotton, gold, lamb, lead, nickel, oil, pig iron, rice, and tin – showed no trend, which, it merits underlining, also implies that *none* of the 25 commodities had improving purchasing power trends in the very long term (Harvey *et al.* 2010:375).

But such long-term trends are certainly not necessary in order to advise against depending on raw materials exports; a decade or two of falling purchasing power should be enough to cause alarm.

One last issue regarding the PSH should be addressed. Looking at the terms-of-trade of primary *commodities* tells us little about the situation of individual *countries* if we do not investigate how dependent each economy is on what resource mix: how much of its imports and exports are primary commodities and industrial goods, respectively. Thus, we may conclude that a country may be dependent on primary commodities but still come out all right in terms of purchasing power, depending on what it exports and what it imports.

This sounds like an important point, but the fact of the matter is that the most influential measure of the terms-of-trade of the *countries* of the Periphery also shows a consistent negative trend, although of a smaller magnitude than the negative trend for primary commodities: the loss of terms-of-trade for *countries* of the Periphery was one-third of the loss suffered by primary commodities in general, still negative although less severely so (Grilli and Yang 1988:35; the conclusion holds for the period 1945–1986). In other words, whether we look at raw materials or at the countries that export them, a negative terms-of-trade trend has been established.

What about the future? If we were to go by earlier boom-bust cycles, we should expect to be entering a new phase of deteriorating terms-of-trade for primary commodities after the speculative price hikes leading up to 2008. However, this pattern is not what we saw in Chapter 2. While admittedly the time period is too short to allow strong conclusions, an unusually fast recuperation of the prices of raw materials and land-based resources (such as food) after the dramatic but brief fall of 2008–2009 has taken place. I attribute this break with the historic pattern of the last hundred years to the new importance of land-based resources for food, feed, fibres and fuels.

There is another reason why the downward trend of primary commodity prices is likely to be over: the rise of new industrial giants is likely to have a major influence on terms-of-trade as they pour cheap industrial goods onto the world market, thus contributing to making deteriorating terms-of-trade of raw materials a thing of the past (Kaplinsky 2006). The logic is simple: the exports of China and others will cause global manufacture prices to fall, making primary commodities (expressed in industrial goods) costlier.

As a result, the PSH will be turned on its head: terms-of-trade will develop to the benefit of the exporters of primary and land-based commodities, just as happened in the period leading up to the financial crisis in 2008, and is happening anew today.

## Unequal exchange of labour

To development economists in the Marxist tradition, Singer's approach does not hold much water: focusing primarily on the goods exchanged, and on market prices, he is criticized for disregarding internal class and power relations, and thus misunderstanding the preconditions for growth and development. One influential representative of this view was economist Paul Baran, who in 1957 dismissed the importance of deteriorating terms-of-trade (in spite of the fact that he recognized that the hypothesis as such could hold true). The problem with giving deteriorating terms-of-trade an important place in the explanation of the divergence between the Centre and the Periphery, according to Baran, was that it could lead us to preferring *improving* terms-of-trade. But higher prices would lead to higher profits, and these were not necessarily to be welcomed, Baran wrote, formulating a warning of what today is called the "resource curse" or the "paradox of plenty":

> [I]t cannot be stressed too strongly that the relevance of the magnitude of profits to the welfare of the peoples inhabiting the underdeveloped countries or to their countries' economic development depends entirely on to whom these profits accrue and on the use which is made of them by their recipients.
>
> (Baran 1967:233)

By implication, deteriorating (or improving) terms-of-trade would not decisively affect the situation one way or the other.

In this political economy strand of development thinking, underdevelopment is primarily caused by internal class relations. Poor countries were poor because the dominating class did not mobilize and make productive use of the surplus that they had access to, Baran stressed, and enumerated four characteristics which explained why the potential of poor countries was not being realized:

> *One* is society's excess consumption (predominantly on the part of the upper income groups ... ), the *second* is the output lost to society through the existence of unproductive workers, the *third* is the output lost because of the irrational and wasteful organization of the existing productive apparatus, and the *fourth* is the output foregone owing to the existence of unemployment caused primarily by the anarchy of capitalist production and the deficiency of effective demand.
>
> (Baran 1967:24)

Not much space for external factors in explaining underdevelopment, it seems. In fact, Baran's approach to development focusses on the domestic relations of power and only pays secondary attention to the international division of labour.

At about the same time, another economist also influenced by the Marxist tradition, Arghiri Emmanuel, constructed a case which combined internal and external circumstances, focusing on the unequal exchange of labour. Emmanuel referred back to Ricardo's stance that trade benefits all trading partners, "a wonderful game, in which each partner has every chance of winning without the slightest risk of losing" in Emmanuel's sarcastic words (Emmanuel 1972:xiii). Emmanuel then sided with the PSH II (i.e. the interpretation of the resource curse which targets the country and not the character of the goods traded) when he stated that the exchange that ought to be studied is that between countries, not the exchange of specific products:

> Are there really certain products that are under a curse, so to speak; or is there, for certain reasons that the dogma of immobility of factors prevents us from seeing, a certain category of countries that, whatever they undertake and whatever the produce, always exchange a larger amount of their national labour for a smaller amount of foreign labour?
>
> (Emmanuel 1972:xxxi)

By the "dogma of immobility of factors" Emmanuel referred to Ricardo's assumption that capital cannot cross borders, quite an important objection to the theory of comparative advantage even then and, of course, more so today.

In sum, it is not the fact that poor countries export agricultural products that explains why they are poor, nor does the fact that rich countries export manufactures explain their wealth. To refute this thought, Emmanuel asserted, "one has only to mention Australia, New Zealand and Denmark, on the one hand, and Spain, Italy and Japan, on the other", implying that primary commodities have been beneficial to the former but not to the latter countries, somewhat illogically including Japan in the ranks of poor exporters of raw materials. Instead, Periphery countries are poor because they have an abundance of labour which keeps wages low, and low wages lead to the use of more labour in the products exported than the products imported. It is a vicious circle breeding underdevelopment and poverty in the Periphery and development and wealth in the Centre, and Emmanuel held that this unequal exchange was the chief mechanism creating an ever-widening gap between Centre and Periphery:

> I think it is possible to state that unequal exchange is the *elementary* transfer mechanism, and that, as such, it enables the advanced countries to begin and regularly to give new impetus to that *unevenness of development* that sets in motion all the other mechanisms of exploitation and fully explains the way that wealth is distributed.
>
> (Emmanuel 1972:265)

Following, Prebisch and Singer as well as Emmanuel, it has become a standard tenet of development economics – Marxist and Keynesian alike – not to accept an international division of labour where the Periphery sticks to primary commodities. The reason is that the objective of development policies is not to achieve maximum efficiency, given a certain distribution of comparative advantages, but rather to improve the position of poor economies in the global division of labour. To put it differently: while Ricardian trade theory accepted the global hierarchy, Keynesian and Marxist economics wanted to change it by introducing a dynamic perspective of evolving "advantages".

The importance of avoiding unequal exchange is underlined by economist Samir Amin, who presented an estimate of what the Periphery would have received from its exports had its labour obtained the same salaries as in the Centre (and had it thus not been relegated to supplying raw materials to the Centre):

> The hidden transfers of value from the periphery to the center, due to the mechanism of unequal exchange, are of the order of $22 billion, that is to say, twice the amount of the "aid" and the private capital that the periphery receives. One is certainly justified in talking of the plundering of the Third World.
>
> (Amin 1976:144)

## Ecologically unequal exchange

In spite of these differences, a common trait of Ricardian trade theory on the one hand, and Marxist and Keynesian on the other, is to view economic growth as tantamount to development. This led Emmanuel to complain that too little land was cultivated, too few rail road lines built, too little cement and steel produced, too few cars. In short, Emmanuel maintained, "our world still largely lies fallow" (Emmanuel 1972:262).

Today, such a lament seems inappropriate, to say the least. The socio-ecological metabolic transition which I discussed in Chapter 1 has resulted in rapidly growing global energy and material flows, leading to a material use which by all indications is far beyond the carrying capacity of most ecological systems (Krausmann *et al.* 2008:652, and MA 2005 for a truly dismal analysis of the state of the world's ecosystems).

That systematic and unequal exchange of land-based resources has taken place for a long time is a trivial proposition in contemporary world system analysis and global environmental justice studies (see Hornborg and Crumley 2007 and Hornborg *et al.* 2007 for representative contributions). But it was only in 1985 with Steven Bunker's influential study of the Brazilian Amazon that an understanding of ecologically unequal exchange began to gain prominence, as he postulated a difference between extractive and productive economies in terms of their opposed "dynamics of scale".

According to Bunker, an extractive economy suffers increasing unit costs of production as it expands, while a productive economy gains from decreasing costs as it grows, hence laying the ground for an unequal exchange between the two. The reason for this imbalance is found in the nature of the economies. While the productive economy becomes more efficient as its scale (i.e. volume of production) increases, the logic works itself out quite differently for extractive economies: "In extractive systems ... unit costs tend to rise as the scale of extraction increases. Greater amounts of any extractive commodity can be obtained only by exploiting increasingly distant or difficult sources" (Bunker 1985:25). There is something strange about the logic here: Bunker's "dis-economies of scale" for raw materials and land-based commodities – as volume increases, unit production cost rises – ought to lead to a tendency for extracted resources to become more expensive (in terms of the industrial goods that they are exchanged for), i.e. the opposite of what the Prebisch–Singer hypothesis (and most of the statistical data) suggest.

This is surprising. The theory which launched the discussion on ecologically unequal exchange could in fact be interpreted in the opposite light: exchanging extracted resources which are becoming more expensive – Bunker's assertion – should benefit countries specializing in such exports when they exchange them for industrial goods which are assumed to become ever cheaper. If this does not in fact take place, we need a theory to explain why.

In his original 1985 study, Bunker did not provide any explanation of why dis-economies of scale do not result in a contrary tendency of unequal exchange to the one he postulates. One answer to this conundrum could be that as long as there are alternative sources for accessing extractive resources, prices may be kept low as corporations abandon old raw material sources once they become difficult or expensive to exploit, and turn to new territories and locations where the ease of access is greater and the costs thus lower. Of course, as resource exploitation progresses around the globe, this solution to Bunker's paradox will reach its own limits in terms of increasing difficulties, and hence increasing costs, of finding primary resources, and a declining terms-of-trade trend will eventually come through.

In a later study, however, Bunker returned to the mystery, this time with a solution: as the growing socio-ecological metabolism has needed raw materials from ever more distant – and hence costly – sources, "capital has responded to this contradiction by increasing the size and speed of transport in ways that reduce the ton-mile cost of moving large volumes of raw material" (Bunker and Ciccantell 2005:xiii). Thus, although an extractive economy suffers from dis-economies of scale as the exploitation of land-based resources is forced to reach over increasing distances, the actual prices do not reflect this logic as it is countered by ever cheaper transports. In other words, the dis-economies of scale of raw materials are made up for by the economies of scale of transports, which accompanied, and facilitated, the colonial and post-colonial appropriation of raw materials.

With this understanding of ecologically unequal exchange, steps taken to secure transport routes are key elements – as I remarked in Chapter 2 – and each phase of imperial domination can be related to a particular transportation strategy. The Dutch, Spanish and Portuguese advanced navigation techniques and built vessels with larger carrying capacities; the British constructed steam-powered ships and trains, and made sure that the infrastructure increased simultaneously; the Suez canal was built, 1859–1869; the US connected the east and west coasts by rail, and opened up the Panama canal, 1904–1914; the Japanese developed bulk transport overseas, a strategy more recently used also by China.

The outcome was that primary commodities were hauled longer and longer distances, an important but disregarded aspect of globalization. In 1960, less than 20 per cent of all iron ore mined was shipped overseas; by 1990, this share had grown to more than 35 per cent, a development propelled especially by resource-poor Japan. Since then, transport has kept on growing: see Table 4.1.

## Concluding remarks

Bunker stresses that countries present "variable mixes of extraction and production" and uses his perspective to "explain the extreme and progressive underdevelopment of the Amazon" (Bunker 1985:13). Thus, his analysis applies primarily to *regional* economies (Hornborg 2007b:8), and ecologically unequal exchange may have as much to tell us about local and intra-national unequal development as about disparities among nations.

Many countries that are seemingly coherent units are in fact split along fault lines: Brazil's south and centre versus its north and northeast, China's coast versus its interior, India's north versus its south. Sweden also displays such a rift south–north, and it goes a long way back. As the Swedish chancellor Axel Oxenstierna is said to have exclaimed when Sweden was a regional power in the early 1600s, pointing toward Norrland, the mineral-rich northern province of Sweden: "Norrland is India within our own borders if only we understand how to make use of it". Bunker himself, however, held that he was complementing Emmanuel's understanding of country trajectories with an ecological dimension of unequal exchange. Towards the end of his study he says: "If we amplify [Emmanuel's] notion about wages to include all measure of unequal exchange,

*Table 4.1* Transport of bulk commodities, *c.*1960 and *c.*2000, tons and per cent change

|  | *c.1960* | *c.2000* | *Per cent change c.1961–c.2000* |
| --- | --- | --- | --- |
| Number of dry bulk carriers | 471 | 5,554 | 1,179 |
| Total tonnage, million dwt | 9 | 290 | 3,200 |
| Transported petroleum, billion ton-miles | 1,650 | 8,180 | 496 |
| Transported iron ore, billion ton-miles | 34 | 2,545 | 7,485 |
| Transported coal, billion ton-miles | 264 | 2,509 | 950 |

Source: Based on Bunker and Ciccantell 2005:217–218.

Note
dwt = dead weight tonnage.

then we can say that *countries* where labor value and natural values are seriously undercompensated will tend indeed to be underdeveloped" (Bunker 1985:252, italics added). On the one hand, this lapse into a national scale is understandable, since almost all available statistics use nations as their unit of analysis; on the other, it is problematic, as national borders may be less than ideal for understanding the actual ecological exchange which takes place, especially some of the more egregious forms of environmental load displacement which I will discuss in Chapter 7.

# 5 Weak and strong measures of the nature–economy interface

Measures to capture the relationship between the economy and nature can be divided into those that assume that economic and natural resources are exchangeable for each other, and those which assume that there is no such substitutability as a rule. Following this distinction, two concepts of sustainability exist, one weak (based on substitutability) and one strong (based on complementarity), each conception associated with a separate discipline, the weak with environmental economics, the strong with ecological economics.

Table 5.1 presents some of the most distinct differences in the world views of these two approaches to the nature–economy interface, environmental versus ecological economics.

Ecological economists maintain that there is a sharp dividing line between themselves and environmental economists, based on the latter group's lack of interest in, not to say ignorance of, natural science. "The basic observation", says ecological economist Inge Röpke in her history of ecological economics as a discipline, is "banal and difficult to disagree with"; "The human economy is embedded in nature, and economic processes are also always natural processes in the sense that they can be seen as biological, physical and chemical processes and transformations" (Röpke 2004:296). But although the banality of this observation may be striking, it nevertheless gives ecological economics its defining

*Table 5.1* Conceptual differences between environmental and ecological economics

|  | *Environmental economics* | *Ecological economics* |
| --- | --- | --- |
| Main concern | Efficiency: the efficient distribution of scarce resources | Scale: the capacity of the ecosystem to sustain the economy |
| Main assumption | Substitutability | Complementarity |
| Conception of sustainability | Weak | Strong |
| Main indicators | Gross domestic product (GDP) corrected for environmental costs (Green GDP) | Physical indicators in relation to ecological carrying capacity |

characteristic, something which is brought home by the fact that two influential and early studies of ecological economics include physical terms in their titles, the entropy law (Georgescu-Roegen 1971) and energy (Martínez-Alier 1990). Similarly, the original 1977 subtitle of Herman Daly's seminal *Steady-State Economics* (1992/1977) reads *The Economics of Biophysical Equilibrium and Moral Growth*. In other words: ecological economics equals biophysical economics (Martínez-Alier 1990:viii).

Thus, while environmental economics is concerned with efficiency and assumes substitutability between economic and ecological resources, ecological economics has a completely different set-up of assumptions and concerns. Most importantly, ecological economics rejects the weak sustainability understanding, where the deficit in one sphere, say nature, can be made up for by surpluses in other spheres, say the economy.

Ecological economics maintains that the various spheres of reality must be measured separately, with metrics which are adapted to the specific traits of each. Not even the economy is captured well by the gross domestic product, GDP, as it only includes market activities and does not differentiate positive from negative components. Deducting a monetary value from the GDP for ecological destruction in order to present the "whole" picture does not improve the situation; on the contrary, efforts to "green" the GDP rather end up making the indicator still weaker and less transparent.

Yet some ecological economists maintain that monetary metrics also have their place, since they transmit the kind of information which political power relates to. Herman Daly once justified using monetary measures when assessing ecosystem services: "for those who only hear dollars, let us scream now and then in dollars!" (Daly 1998:23). A study which follows Daly's recommendation compares the countries which cause environmental destruction to the ones that suffer from it. The environmental damages considered were climate change, ozone-layer depletion, agricultural intensification and expansion, deforestation, overfishing, and mangrove loss, and the time horizon extends to the end of the twenty-first century; see Table 5.2.

Table 5.2 shows how low-income countries have to endure more than "their share" of the overall ecological damages, and high-income countries less. In

*Table 5.2* Distribution of ecological loads caused 1961–2000 and suffered until 2100

|  | Low-income countries | Middle-income countries | High-income countries |
|---|---|---|---|
| Share of population 1961–2000, % | 32 | 50 | 18 |
| Share of damages caused, % | 14 | 58 | 28 |
| Share of damages suffered, % | 20 | 60 | 20 |
| Share of damages suffered when human lives are equally valued, % | 45 | 52 | 3 |

Source: Based on Srinivasan *et al.* 2008.

other words, the distribution of the drivers causing ecological destruction and the monetized costs of suffering from this destruction is biased against the poor countries: low-income countries accounted for 14 per cent of the causes but suffered 20 per cent of the consequences.

Some would be alarmed by this gap, and others would probably be surprised that it is not wider; I belong to the latter group. The reason why the disparities are so small is a double weakness in the design of the calculation. First, causes are attributed to the countries where they are "produced", not to the countries where they are "consumed", but, as I will discuss further in Chapter 6, a significant share of pollution in low-income countries is caused when producing goods for the high-income countries. Thus, an even larger part of the causes ought to be attributed to the high-income countries than shown in Table 5.2, leaving a concomitantly smaller responsibility for the drivers with the low-income countries.

Second, damages are valued according to the GDP per capita, which means that impact in rich countries, and on rich people, is valued higher than equal damages to poor countries and their populations. The study recognizes this drawback, however, and uses purchasing power parity (PPP) data to soften the value-judgement implied by valuing people according to their income. Although this is a step in the right direction, it does not change the fact that the methodology is flawed in equity terms: by using PPP you only reduce the imbalance, you do not erase it.

Had the study on which Table 5.2 is based used instead what it calls an "equity weighting" – i.e. assessed human beings as equally valuable in monetary terms – the low-income group would have carried more than twice the burden it does with the present valuation. As a consequence, the injustice would have come across much more strongly, with low-income countries suffering three times the damages that they themselves cause, 45 and 14 per cent, respectively; see the last row of Table 5.2. For the high-income countries, this equity logic gives the opposite result: with equity weighting, high-income countries would only suffer 3 per cent of the damage while they account for 28 per cent of the causes.

Furthermore, the study uses net present values – with a discount factor of 2 per cent – which reduces the value of future generations compared with the present one; thus the model is also biased in generational terms.

Many ecological measures – although expressed in physical terms – also try to find one sole indicator for the ecological sphere as a whole, which opens them up to the objection that they measure incommensurable ecological states. They are thus reductionist but strong in the sustainability dimension. This is what happens when we express a number of ecological concerns in one measure – hectares, litres or tons, for instance – to indicate their ecological weight.

It should be recognized that reductionism brings advantages by allowing complex and contradictory tendencies to be expressed in simple figures, yielding an impression of clarity. The most successful of these simplified measures is the GDP, which in the public domain serves as indicator of wealth and development in addition to its purported value as a measure of the level of economic activity;

on the other hand, non-reductionist indicators run up against the difficulty of presenting easy-to-grasp summaries of the state of nature.

The Millennium Ecosystem Assessment, MA, exemplifies the strength and weakness of the non-reductionist sustainability approach. The MA analysed 24 ecosystems – called life supporting systems – divided into three groups: provisioning services, e.g. food and fibres; regulating services, e.g. climate and water; and cultural services, e.g. tourism and spiritual values. These systems are neither substitutable for each other, nor for services or goods provided by the economy; none of the services is valued in monetary terms; and the MA does not attempt to present an overall summary picture. The conclusion therefore is limited to the alarming but rather general statement that "approximately 60% (15 out of 24) of the ecosystem services examined … are being degraded or used unsustainably" (MA 2005:16). The approach of the MA goes against the grain in environmental economics of assigning monetary value to environmental services, but it also questions the trend in ecological economics of finding easily understandable macro-indicators for the nature–economy interface.

## Measures of ecological exchange

My prime concern is to measure the exchange of land areas and land-based resources in order to assess the extent to which ecologically unequal exchange is taking place in the global economy. Five measures will be used. As I have just noted, physical indicators are appealing to ecological economists as they avoid the assumption of weak sustainability, although they still may suffer from reductionism.

### *Ecological footprints*

Ecological footprints (EF) measure "the amount of biologically productive land and water area an individual, a city, a country, a region, or all of humanity uses to produce the resources it consumes and to absorb the carbon dioxide emissions it generates" (Global Footprint Network 2012a). Land areas appropriated are calculated as the sum of the areas occupied for renewable resources – forests, crop lands, fisheries and grazing lands – plus a hypothetical land area for the absorption of carbon emissions, all expressed in "global hectares", glha, with average land productivity.

This procedure implies that various lands are substitutable for each other, which entails a certain reductionism, as many land areas in fact cannot perform the same ecological functions; to use my previous terminology, land areas are not perfectly fungible. But, as I also argued, they are sufficiently fungible to allow us to use concepts as encompassing as global hectares. More controversial, perhaps, is that the EF includes an area for fish catch, where the fungibility is questionable (Borgström Hansson 2003:167–168).

A problematic aspect of the EF approach from the point of view of measuring the exchange of land areas is the fact that the carbon component of the footprint is a measure of hypothetical $CO_2$ absorption and does not measure actual land use (in contrast to the other components of the footprint, except the fish footprint, which shares this weakness). In the early 1990s, when the footprint methodology was being elaborated, two ways to calculate a "fossil footprint" were discussed: one option was to use the land area needed to grow agrofuels to replace fossil fuels; another was to calculate the land area needed to absorb the carbon dioxide that was emitted from the use of fossil fuels.

In the end, as we have seen, the latter method was chosen, as the consequences of using the absorption areas were seen to be conservative compared to using agrofuel land area equivalents. The land area needed to absorb the carbon dioxide from 100 GJ (100 billion joule) was set at one hectare; if that land area instead had been used to grow feedstocks for ethanol, it would only have yielded 80 GJ. Thus, by choosing the hypothetical carbon sequestration figure, the EF is smaller than it would have been, had the land area for equivalent ethanol production been used (Wackernagel and Rees 1996:72–74).

Today, however, and using Brazilian techniques and land yields, the equivalent sugar cane area is smaller, and introducing Brazilian sugarcane data – with yields of 139 GJ per hectare – would give a smaller footprint than the one used by the EF (see Table 8.1 below). Still, the EF may also today be seen as a conservative estimate of the actual human appropriation of renewable land-based resources, as there are interpretations of the fossil footprint which lead to including still larger areas, such as calculating the area of the *past* bio-capacity embodied in today's fossil fuels (Kitzes *et al.* 2007:6).

Another contentious issue is how to account for nuclear power. Initially, the footprint of nuclear power was calculated as the land area that would have been needed to absorb the emissions of $CO_2$ from an equivalent volume of electricity produced by fossil fuels. But since actual fossil fuel electricity production units had very different efficiency levels, no reliable estimate of the relevant ecologically productive land area could be calculated. This is the reason for deleting the nuclear power footprint given by the Living Planet Report of 2008. For a nuclear-dependent country such as Sweden, omitting the nuclear power footprint has reduced the total EF of Sweden by as much as 14 per cent, from 6.1 glha to 5.1 glha from 2003 to 2005 (WWF 2008).

In any case, the EF only accounts for part of the total human footprint – renewable resources and carbon emissions – and then compares this with the total land areas available, without taking account of the needs of other species in terms of ecologically productive areas. This is part of the claim for relevancy that the approach presents: if humankind alone is overusing the available land area without accounting for the needs of competing species, the real predicament of making human lifestyles fit within the available space is exacerbated.

But leaving out non-human demand for land may give an impression that the appropriation of land areas is less serious than it is. For instance, when the Global Footprint Network, GFN, concludes that human needs are 151 per cent of the available renewable resources, this is in fact a serious understatement, as it leaves out the needs of all other species apart from humans. Similarly, when the

GFN calculates the global overshoot day – 22 August 2012 – and concludes that it tends to arrive a few days earlier each year, the actual overshoot takes place earlier still if all demands for the ecological resources were accounted for (Global Footprint Network 2012b).

## *Water footprints*

The water footprint (WF) of a nation is calculated in analogy with the Ecological footprint, using three sources of water: rainwater (called green water); use of ground or surface water for irrigation (blue water); and a measure of water pollution estimated by the volume of clean water needed to dilute polluted water to acceptable standards (grey water; Hoekstra and Chapagain 2008, Hoekstra and Mekonnen 2012). Grey water is not used water but a hypothetical volume, similar to the land areas estimated for the absorption of $CO_2$ emissions included in the EF.

## *Physical trade balances*

A measure of the impact of the economy on the environment that is gaining increasing currency is materials flow analysis (MFA). The measure consists of four material flows which are aggregated: construction minerals, ores and industrial minerals, fossil energy, and biomass (compare Figure 1.1 above). From the MFA data, I use the traded goods, expressed as physical trade balances, PTB.

The PTB is suitable for measuring resource flows across borders, as we here calculate actual transported volumes, but its composition makes it less than ideal for capturing the ecological significance of these flows. In fact, MFA and PTB reduce ecological load to one common physical indicator – tons – and does not differentiate among its constituent parts; consider the implication of putting mercury on an equal footing with sand and concluding that the small flow of mercury constitutes less of an ecological problem than the much larger flows of sand (Adriaanse *et al.* 1997: 6).

One response to this weakness of the MFA is to abandon all ambitions to use it as an *ecological* indicator and simply see it as "'value-neutral' physical accounts that include all materials, regardless of their economic importance or environmental impact" (Mathews *et al.* 2000:2). Other proponents of MFA also recognize the problem: "we must ask whether the total weight of materials processed by a socioeconomic system is a viable indicator for 'environmental impact' at all" (Amann *et al.* 2002:6). The authors respond to their own query in the affirmative, although not very convincingly. Assuming, they write, that technology remains fixed and does not change, then "increases in resource input imply increase in environmental impact" (ibid.). But the assumption is unrealistic: as Friedrich Engels was already asking in 1844, why would technical change suddenly stop?

Another drawback of the MFA is that it excludes two material flows which are central from an ecological point of view, water and air emissions, on account of their huge volumes. The reason is simple: had they been included, the other four components of the MFA would have been dwarfed. This is perhaps under-standable, but it does not reinforce the ecological significance of the MFA.

## Human appropriation of net primary production

While material flow analysis and water footprints measure the socio-ecological metabolism in physical terms, they do not – unlike the ecological footprint – relate it to a "limit of growth" discourse. But there is another physical measure which aids us in establishing how far away, or indeed how close, we are to over-loading the natural systems supporting the economy. This is the human appro-priation of net primary production (HANPP), a measure which estimates the share of available ecological resources that the economy uses.

The point of departure is the *potential* net primary product of land measured via satellite images, normally in areas of 10 km by 10 km, and calculated in an appropriate physical metric, here the carbon flow per year. From this indicator, the *actual* available net primary product today is deducted; the difference consti-tutes the HANPP. In other words, the actual available net primary product is what remains for all other uses and users on Earth after humans have had their share (Vitousek *et al.* 1986, Haberl *et al.* 2007).

Estimates of the global HANPP varies, from the highest and most frequently quoted, 40 per cent (Vitousek *et al.* 1986:373), to the most recent figure, 22 per cent (Haberl *et al.* 2007:7). In other words, humans appropriate 22 to 40 per cent of the potentially available net primary production on Earth, leaving only 60 to 78 per cent to all remaining species and ecosystem functions. These HANPP figures are stated for the world as a whole, but the regional distribution is extremely uneven and does not follow national borders or income categories. The HANPP is in fact closely cor-related with population density. This gives us another indication that ecologically unequal exchange is not always meaningfully captured by national data.

With HANPP we once more – as when considering ecological footprints – encounter the possibility of relating human appropriation to "sustainability thresholds", to the absolute capacity of the natural system to sustain the economy. In the case of the EF, we related the appropriation of the economy to the total available areas; in relation to HANPP, it is the total available net primary product which constitutes the ultimate limit for the expansion of the economy. Still, it is not easy to know where the acceptable threshold for HANPP should be put. It should be clear that 100 per cent HANPP would be destructive, as no space is left for species other than humans, but what about 22 per cent, or 40? (See Haberl *et al.* 2004 for a comparison of HANPP and EF.)

## Carbon footprints

Carbon footprints (CF) have gained increasing attention for reasons related to climate politics and to the discussion about environmental load displacement. The Kyoto Protocol deals with domestic emissions of greenhouse gases, but a significant part of the emissions which occur in any given economy comes from the production of goods for export: should not those emissions be attributed to the countries whose demand set the factory wheels spinning, rather than to the countries where the goods were manufactured?

If we let the place of production constitute the point of recording of the emissions, we are likely to hold the Periphery responsible for specializing in carbon-intensive products, while the importing countries of the Centre will appear to be less of a problem for the climate (Peters *et al.* 2011). By measuring how carbon emissions of an economy are used for domestic consumption and exports, respectively, while also taking into account the carbon emitted to produce the goods imported to each country, the comparison allows us to calculate the net balance in embodied traded carbon.

## Concluding remarks

Four of the five measures which I will use in the next chapter to assess ecologically unequal exchange – ecological footprints, water footprints, HANPP, and carbon footprints – have an important feature in common: they capture the *embodied* ecological content of the goods, not what they actually contain when they cross the borders. What we can see or measure in terms of area or water or carbon content of the goods traded is only a small part of the ecological resources which actually went into producing them. In other words, we have to impute these values by estimating the resources which were used up along the production chain. Our measures are thus *embodied* hectares, litres and tons.

On the other hand, the physical trade balance, which gives the actual weights of traded goods, in fact only indicates part of the total, as the *indirect* weight is unaccounted for. For instance, when we weigh the exports of copper from Chile or Zambia, only the weight of the refined copper which passes the border is included, not the much heavier loads which were deposited domestically along the route from the mine to the port. In this sense, the PTB is (partly) a disembodied measure of ecologically unequal exchange.

More to the point for my investigation of the role of land areas and land-based resources is how the varying indicators capture the aspect of traded "land": see Table 5.3. With my purpose of measuring ecologically unequal exchange of land areas, the water and carbon footprints (WF and CF) stand out as the least useful.

*Table 5.3* A comparison of measures of ecological exchange

| Measure | Ecological relevance | Transfer of resources | Land relevance | Availability of data |
|---------|---------------------|----------------------|----------------|---------------------|
| EF | high | embodied | high | low |
| WF | high | embodied | low | low |
| PTB | low | real | medium | high |
| HANPP | high | embodied | high | low |
| CF | high | embodied | low | low |

Comparing the various measures on the basis of one specific application of them – to gauge ecologically unequal exchange – should however not be taken as an overall assessment of their usefulness or relevance; the indicators are different precisely because they have been devised with different purposes in mind. For instance, the HANPP is spatially specific when it measures human appropriation of net primary production on a given territory; the EF, on the other hand, while providing such thresholds – either in relation to global standards or in relation to national land areas – does not provide locally relevant thresholds, but rather captures the ecological overshoot, that is, the appropriation of global resources.

Thus we are left with measures which are far from ideal, yet sufficiently illuminating, I believe, to enable us to say something interesting and relevant about ecologically unequal exchange in an effort to understand the general phenomenon of appropriation of ecological space.

# 6   Measures and interpretations of ecologically unequal exchange

It is now time to use the five measures I discussed in the previous chapter, which combine physical indicators and a strong understanding of sustainability, both necessary requisites in order to be ecologically meaningful and usable to assess ecologically unequal exchange, EUE.

## Measuring ecologically unequal exchange

A word of caution before we start. When estimating EUE, imports of ecological resources are seen as positive and exports as negative, the opposite of what we are used to thinking when considering trade flows (where exports of goods and services are positive, and imports negative). However, in ecological terms, and this is what counts here, imports allow a country to access ecological resources, while exports signify that a country gives up ecological resources. Hence,

EUE = ecological imports − ecological exports

A negative EUE signifies that a country is sending away more ecological resources than it is receiving; a positive EUE implies that a country is obtaining more ecological resources from the exchange than it is losing.

Following the theory of ecologically unequal exchange discussed in Chapter 4, a simple hypothesis may be formulated: the sign of the EUE is positive for economies of the Centre (or North) and negative for economies of the Periphery (or South), as an unequal distribution of power and wealth translates into an unequal ecological exchange. This is the hypothesis which will now be tested.

### Measure 1: Ecological footprints

In Figure 6.1 I have calculated the EUE for 2006 with the help of ecological footprints. Compare Chile, China, and Brazil to the US and Japan for the clearest differences: Chile, China, and Brazil have large negative EUE, the US and Japan large positive EUE. This pattern substantiates my hypothesis: the Centre is appropriating ecological resources from the Periphery.

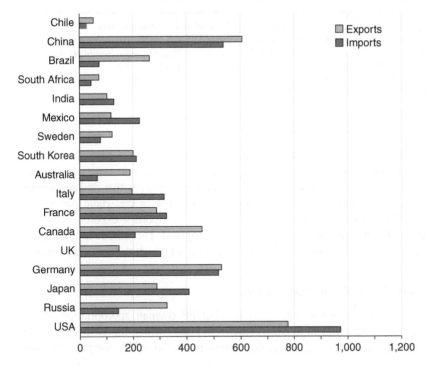

*Figure 6.1* Ecological footprints of trade, 2006, million global hectares; the countries
included are the 13 major trading nations and the most recently joined members
of the OECD (Chile, Mexico, and South Korea), plus Sweden (author's calculation; data from Global footprint network, www.globalfootprint.org/).

However, there are exceptions, and they indicate that countries which are
relatively resource-rich, such as Sweden, Canada and Australia, have negative
balances, yet on all other counts belong to the Centre.

### *Measure 2: Water footprints*

The water footprint follows the trade of agricultural products quite closely,
explaining the pattern of water exchange, where the large food and feed crops
exporters have negative water balances, while we find agricultural importers on
the positive side; see Table 6.1.

Thus, there is EUE, but it does not comply with the traditional division of the
globe as Centre/Periphery (or North/South). On the contrary, water footprint balances indicate that arid regions gain from trade.

*Table 6.1* Water footprint balances of world regions, average 1995–1999

| | |
|---|---|
| Higly positive EUE | Western Europe, Central Asia, Southern Asia |
| Moderately positive EUE | Middle East, Northern Africa, Central Africa, Southern Africa |
| Highly negative EUE | North America, South America, Oceania, Southeast Asia |
| Moderately negative EUE | Central America, Russia, Eastern Europe |

Source: Based on Hoekstra and Hung 2005, Figure 2.

## Measure 3: Physical trade balances

Physical trade balances (PTB) for the last 40 years are given for industrialized, transition, and developing countries in Figure 6.2. For the nine points in time for which PTB has been calculated, industrial countries have a positive, and developing countries a negative PTB. The pattern is consistent over the whole period: the North's PTB has been growing ever more positive (imports > exports), while the South's PTB has remained negative (exports > imports). The balance is made up by transition economies, which show increasing deficits towards the end of the period.

## Measure 4: HANPP of traded biomass

I have only come across one study of HANPP (human appropriation of net primary production), dealing with trade in biomass, where the EUE is possible to measure; see Table 6.2. Here, the pattern is similar to the one portrayed for

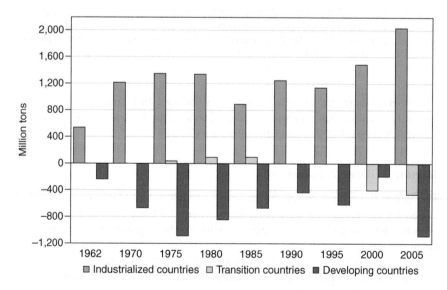

*Figure 6.2* Physical trade balances of industrialised, transition and developing countries, 1962–2005, million tons; the positive and negative flows do not balance out, which indicates data weakness (source: Dittrich and Bringezu 2010:1846, used with permission).

*Table 6.2* Share of embodied HANPP in biomass trade, 2000, percentages

| Net exporters (negative EUE) | Share of global embodied HANPP in biomass exports, % | Net importers (positive EUE) | Share of global embodied HANPP in biomass imports, % |
|---|---|---|---|
| USA | 23 | Japan | 13 |
| Australia | 15 | China | 8 |
| Argentina | 14 | Netherlands | 6 |
| Brazil | 12 | South Korea | 6 |
| Canada | 11 | Mexico | 5 |
| Thailand | 4 | Italy | 5 |
| Kazakhstan | 3 | Belgium-Luxembourg | 4 |
| Ukraine | 2 | Germany | 4 |
| Malaysia | 1 | UK | 4 |
| France | 1 | Spain | 4 |

Source: Erb *et al.* 2009b, Table 1.

the water footprint (see Table 6.1 above), and no clear Centre/Periphery divide is discernible: net agricultural exporters are net suppliers of HANPP (i.e. have negative EUE, as seen in the left side of Table 6.2), while densely populated countries are large net importers (positive EUE, right side).

### *Measure 5: Carbon footprint*

Table 6.3 gives net embodied emissions of $CO_2$ for countries of the Kyoto Protocol. In general, the EUE hypothesis is confirmed: the sign of the balance shifts with the position of the economy in the global system. The Centre (Annex B) is net importing of $CO_2$, and the Periphery (Non-Annex B) net exporting of $CO_2$, just as the EUE hypotheses suggests; compare, as before, USA and China. As a whole, a little more than 20 per cent of domestic emissions are for exports (Peters and Hertwich 2008: Figure 1).

With this measure too, there are exceptions: several resource-rich Annex-B countries have negative EUE, for instance Australia, Canada and Russia. But overall, Annex B countries show positive, and Non-Annex B countries negative, EUE.

### *Summing up: gauging ecologically unequal exchange*

With most of the measures and indicators I have applied, we find the expected pattern of ecologically unequal exchange: the Centre, taken as a whole, imports more ecological resources than it exports, while the opposite holds for the Periphery; see Table 6.4. The iconic economies in this summary are Brazil and Japan, representing the ideal pattern of the Periphery and Centre, respectively.

However, most indicators also show that there is more than one relationship of EUE. Tables 6.5 and 6.6 illustrate the more complex picture for a number of countries of the Centre as well as of the Periphery.

The number of cases to substantiate the existence of EUE in favour of the Centre is convincing. The few exceptions in the Centre are sparsely populated countries with large land areas and abundant land-based resources, either agriculture or minerals or both, which have negative EUE (most consistently Australia and Canada).

One thing that is clear from the way the various indicators are constructed is that they understate the phenomenon of EUE, and furthermore present it in a skewed manner. First, measures of footprints of traded goods make brave assumptions as to the production techniques of different countries in order to be able to estimate "embodied" ecological content. Since more information is available from the Centre than from the Periphery, there is a tendency to apply data from the former to the latter (a procedure known as domestic technology assumption, DTA). This results in an underestimation of the "embodied" footprints of quite serious dimensions, as the relative energy and resource use is greater in the Periphery than in the Centre (on account of newer and more resource-efficient equipment as well as stricter environmental regulations in the Centre compared to the Periphery).

Table 6.3 EUE by balance of embodied $CO_2$ emissions in trade, percentage of domestic emissions, 2001

| Annex B | EUE, % | Non-Annex B | EUE, % |
|---|---|---|---|
| USA | +8 | China | −18 |
| Russia | −22 | Middle East | −13 |
| Japan | +15 | India | −7 |
| Germany | +16 | Korea | +11 |
| UK | +17 | Mexico | +5 |
| Canada | −3 | Former Soviet Union excluding Russia | −13 |
| France | +16 | South Africa | −38 |
| Italy | +15 | Brazil | −1 |
| Belarus/Ukraine | −13 | Indonesia | −19 |
| Australia | −17 | Taiwan | −3 |
| Poland | −9 | Turkey | −4 |
| Spain | +10 | Thailand | −14 |
| Netherlands | +19 | Venezuela | −20 |
| Belgium | +44 | Argentina | −2 |
| Czech Republic | −15 | Malaysia | −20 |
| Greece | +6 | | |
| Finland | −9 | | |
| Denmark | +14 | | |
| Portugal | +14 | | |
| Sweden | +40 | | |
| Rest of Annex B | +20 | Rest of Non-Annex B | +17 |
| Annex B | +6 | Non-Annex B | −8 |

Source: Peters and Hertwich (2008):1404.

Note
Countries are listed in order of domestic emissions of $CO_2$.

Table 6.4 Measuring ecologically unequal exchange

| Country/region | Ecological footprint, 2006 | Water footprint/year, 1997–2001 | PTB, various years | HANPP of biomass, 2000 | Carbon footprint, 2001 |
|---|---|---|---|---|---|
| **Periphery** | | | | | |
| Brazil | negative | Latin America negative; Africa and Asia positive | negative | mixed | negative |
| China | negative | negative | negative | negative | negative |
| India | negative | negative | positive | positive | negative |
| | positive | negative | positive | balanced | negative |
| **Centre** | positive | North America, Australia negative; Europe and Japan positive | positive | mixed | positive |
| EU | positive | positive | positive | positive | positive |
| Germany | balanced | positive | positive | positive | positive |
| Japan | positive | positive | positive | positive | positive |
| USA | positive | negative | negative | negative | positive |
| Sweden | negative | positive | negative | negative | positive |

Note
Positive EUE: Imports>Exports; Negative EUE: Exports>Imports.
The table replicates the information presented in this chapter, with additions.

*Table 6.5* Ecological footprints: rule and exception, 2006

| Rule: periphery with negative balance | Exception: periphery with positive balance | Exception: centre with negative balance | Rule: centre with positive balance |
|---|---|---|---|
| China, Brazil, Chile, South Africa | India | Australia, Canada, Sweden | Italy, France, UK, Japan, USA |

Note
Based on Figure 6.1.

For instance, in the case of Norway, the import of $CO_2$ becomes 2.5 times larger with real technology factors than when relying on DTA (Peters and Hertwich 2006:97). Similarly, estimates for the Swedish economy from 2000 to 2005 indicate that Swedish embodied imports are three times as large with the actual production data as when sticking to the DTA (Carlsson-Kanyama *et al.* 2007:19). The imbalance in terms of embodied footprints is thus likely to be even greater compared to what the figures and tables in this chapter have shown (Andrew *et al.* 2009).

Secondly, there is the issue of indirect flows, i.e. the resources which go into a product before it crosses the border. Ideally, as discussed above, indirect flows should be included in order to account for the whole production chain. As of now, however, such information is only available from a few studies, but we may still presume that the material flows which I have used most likely underestimate the actual EUE in favour of the North. A couple of examples indicate how important the issue is (Eisenmenger 2008:169; Weisz 2007; Giljum and Eisenmenger 2004):

*Table 6.6* Water footprint: top ten (plus Sweden) net exporters and net importers, 1997–2001, Gm³/year

| Net exporters | EUE (Imp-Exp) Gm³ | Net importers | EUE (Imp-Exp) Gm³ |
|---|---|---|---|
| Australia | −64 | Japan | +92 |
| Canada | −60 | Italy | +51 |
| USA | −53 | UK | +47 |
| Argentina | −45 | Germany | +35 |
| Brazil | −45 | South Korea | +32 |
| Ivory Coast | −33 | Mexico | +29 |
| Thailand | −28 | Hong Kong | +27 |
| India | −25 | Iran | +15 |
| Ghana | −18 | Spain | +14 |
| Ukraine | −17 | Saudi Arabia | +13 |
| | | Sweden | +6 |

Source: Chapagain and Hoekstra 2004:46.

Note
Gm³ = 1 billion m³ = 1 trillion litres.

• Denmark shows twice as high material flows when including indirect flows as when they are left out.
• The weight of Chile's copper exports would increase 13-fold if we included the indirect flows, thus making Chile's physical trade balance much more negative than normally shown.
• US imports are four times as heavy when the indirect flows are included as in the usual PTB.

These cases indicate that indirect flows are large, and that including them would reinforce the Centre/Periphery inequity in resource flows. For instance, Germany's imports carry indirect flows which are six times as heavy as the ones reported, while their exports "only" have five times as heavy indirect flows (average figures 2000–2007). This means that by including all indirect flows for Germany, its exports as well as its imports, its PTB will be still more positive than it already is, thus reinforcing its EUE surplus (Buyny and Lauber 2010:14 and Table 1).

The same holds for indirect flows concerning the USA, Ecuador, Mexico, Brazil, Chile and Colombia: indirect flows from the Periphery to the Centre carry heavier indirect loads, in most cases, than the opposite flow from the Centre to the Periphery (Muñoz Jaramillo 2011).

In conclusion, the DTA as well as the non-inclusion of indirect flows reduce the magnitude of the EUE and the surpluses appropriated by the Centre. As imports to the Centre carry a heavier indirect rucksack than the opposite flow, and as the techniques actually used in the Periphery are more resource-intensive than those of the Centre, the "real" positive EUE of the Centre is still more marked than I have indicated. Similarly for the Periphery, its "real" negative EUE is even greater than the used indicators disclose. As of today, therefore, the appropriation of ecological resources by the Centre is underreported.

## Where does EUE lead?

It seems to me that the overall conclusion is that we ought to consider a combination of circumstances when discussing EUE: the position of an economy in the global system, the population density, and its endowment with raw materials and other land-based resources.

Countries harbouring raw materials, especially if their land areas are large, have a tendency to be net exporters of embodied ecological areas/tons/litres, irrespective of their position in the global hierarchy (Brazil, Canada, Australia, and Sweden); while the balance is positive for countries with few land-based resources but with lots of people, if they are wealthy (Japan and Western Europe being the typical cases). In fact all of the 27 members of the European Union have a positive PTB except Latvia and Sweden (Eurostat 2011:3).

Furthermore, it has recently been shown that there are at least three patterns when it comes to EUE for today's fast-growing economies (Dittrich *et al.* 2011). Some of the fast-growing economies show distinctly negative PTB, for instance

Russia, Brazil and South Africa; while others, such as China and South Korea, have strongly positive PTB. In between these clear-cut groups, there are also fast-growing economies with more less balanced PTB, such as India. Does this mean that the question regarding the importance of EUE has to be left open, as development (conventionally measured) pathways show both positive and negative EUE patterns?

I believe that we can be a bit more specific when it comes to advocating a development strategy based on land areas and land-based resources, by introducing a temporal aspect. Over time, land-based strategies depend on sustainable resource use, or expanding resource frontiers, either within the borders of the economies themselves (relevant for large countries) or in the global system as a whole; it is this latter exchange that the metrics applied here have captured.

What is possible for individual economies, however, is impossible for an expanding global socio-ecological metabolism as a whole: the fuelling of a process of continuous accumulation will run up against the absolute resource limits (peak oil, peak soil) which I have postulated.

### *Recommendation I: Increase efficiency*

One conclusion drawn in the literature on ecologically unequal exchange is that we should look for a more "optimal" and "efficient" allocation of production in order to minimize the footprints, in arguments reminiscent of the large-scale transfer of the Earth's agriculture which I discussed in Chapter 2. For instance, we are encouraged to consider shifting agriculture to reduce the water footprint "from land areas with low water productivity to land areas with high water productivity, thus increasing global water use efficiency" (Hoekstra and Chapagain 2008:63). Through trade, 5 per cent of the water footprint in agriculture is saved; without these trade flows, more water would have been used in agriculture. This is not a self-evident conclusion from the water footprint approach; as its proponents recognize, shifting consumption patterns to less meat would be much more important for saving water, but such a route is ruled out as unfeasible "since the worldwide trend has been for meat consumption to increase rather than decrease" (Hoekstra and Chapagain 2008:63). This is yet another example of the reluctance to discuss lifestyle issues, to be added to the cases I discussed in Chapter 2.

A similar interpretation in favour of efficiency from the field of physical trade balances states that meat ought to be produced where the feed factor weighs the least. As the weight of the feed needed for meat production in Europe is ten times the weight of the resulting meat, while the global average is only four times, the conclusion is given: to import meat from the South to the North "reduces the material input" (Eisenmenger 2008:169). Likewise, analysis of the carbon footprint may lead to the conclusion that production ought to "occur where it is environmentally preferable and then trade the products internationally" (Peters and Hertwich 2008:1403).

In other words, measures of EUE may result in an efficiency argument, not necessarily in a discussion of equity and unequal distribution of benefits and costs, not to speak of issues related to power in relation to control over land and land-based resources. Again, the reasoning is similar to the global scenarios we came across in Chapter 2, which appeared to aim at making land available for the production of agrofuels by transferring agriculture – although perhaps not the peasants – to countries better suited than the lands where agriculture is actually practiced today.

### Recommendation II: Increase self-reliance

But inter-dependency may also be interpreted as a threat. We encountered this argument in Chapter 1 when considering the historic conflicts over access to land areas and land-based resources. The danger of dependency affects countries of the Centre as well as of the Periphery, and while the logic analysed in Chapter 1 pushed land-resource dependent countries of the Centre towards *securing* their access by any means available, from trade to war, a different logic leads to *reducing* the dependency by going in the direction of self-reliance.

For example, the US is importing large land areas of forestry and agricultural produce, the equivalent of the combined surfaces of Germany, Italy, Spain and the United Kingdom. In these exchanges, it is argued, natural resources become "a factor in geopolitical security" (Kissinger and Rees 2010:596). To David Ricardo in 1817, as we have seen, such inter-dependencies were to be welcomed as they reduced conflicts and rivalries. But now we are advised to limit trade and head in the direction of self-sufficiency, a route which probably resonates better in large and resource-rich, than in small and resource-poor, countries: "all countries should protect or restore their own natural capital and enhance their self-reliance" (Kissinger and Rees 2009:2314). So, there are two ways of reducing the potential conflict arising from the ever-growing exchange of land areas and land-based resources: more trade (Recommendation I), and less trade (Recommendation II).

### Recommendation III: Consumption trumps production

It is clear that, historically, the responsibility for global warming rests with the Centre, a fact which is underlined by the key principle "common but differentiated responsibilities", CBD, stated in the preamble of the Climate convention of 1992 and repeated in the 1997 Kyoto Protocol, Article 10. The CBD principle recognizes that although countries of the world have a common responsibility to counter global warming, the weight of this responsibility falls differently upon the signatories of the UN Framework Convention on Climate Change (UNFCCC): in the Kyoto Protocol, CBD was interpreted as requiring no reductions of greenhouse gas (GHG) emissions in countries of the South (so-called Non-Annex B countries, see Table 6.3). This interpretation was carried forward in the Doha agreement on prolonging Kyoto until 2020 (UNFCCC 2012).

But while common but differential responsibilities may have been a precondition for getting countries of the South to sign the convention and later the protocol, it has now become a blockage for a new post-Kyoto agreement, as the previous understanding of what CBD means is no longer acceptable to the North. The stalling of the climate negotiations since the Conference of the Parties at Copenhagen 2009 (COP 15) indicates, at least to me, that the difficulty of tackling the production–consumption contradiction is one of the key blocks on the road to a new protocol. As long as the Annex I (or Annex B according to Kyoto) countries accept only the production perspective, the South (especially fast-growing and exporting economies such as China, India, Brazil and South Africa) will refuse every binding commitment to reduce their emissions, which, as we have seen, are increasingly caused by their export production: over a fifth of national emissions, on average, arise from production to meet demand from international markets.

However, a consumption perspective might contribute to overcoming this impasse by allocating the responsibility for the emissions not to the producing but to the consuming economy. The ranking of the world's top two polluters is inverted when the logic changes from production to consumption: with a production measure of emissions, China was the leading polluter in the world 2008, and the US was second; with a consumption perspective, it was the other way around (Peters *et al.* 2011:25 and Figure S11).

Passing from a production to a consumption logic thus enables us to allocate the responsibility for global environmental loads differently by pinning emissions to the end-use, the real driver of the production which caused the emissions. For countries of the Organization for Economic Cooperation and Development (OECD) in general, emissions computed on a consumption basis rose more quickly than when measuring production, while for Brazil, Russia, India, China and South Africa – the so called BRICS – the trend is the opposite: their production-based emissions have increased faster than their own consumption emissions. In other words, BRICS are *increasingly* polluting on behalf of the world market. And, concomitantly, the OECD is *increasingly* appropriating ecological space through its trade.

Not only does computing the total consumption footprint lead to a change in the ranking of countries, it may also alter the performance of individual countries. Take Sweden as a case in point once more: Sweden's officially reported production figures of GHG diverge more and more from those obtained when using a consumption-based analysis. While production data indicate a decrease, albeit small, of Swedish emissions of greenhouse gases, consumption-based data on the contrary show that Sweden increased its GHG emissions by as much as 20 per cent from 1993 to 2005 (Berglund 2011:67). Per capita, Swedish emissions of $CO_2$ doubles, from six tons (production) to 12 tons (consumption; Carlsson-Kanyama *et al.* 2007:29). The conclusion is that far from an absolute decoupling of economic growth from GHG, Sweden has transferred emissions abroad via international trade, thus following the general pattern of the economies of the Centre.

## Concluding remarks

Summing up, and using the various indicators presented above, the *general* pattern is one of ecologically unequal exchange, leading to an appropriation of ecological space by the Centre. But there are exceptions to this rule. Some economies are expanding fast although their EUE is negative (from Chile and Brazil to China); others have grown rich although they are dependent on raw materials exports (from Sweden to Australia and Canada); and yet others with positive EUE do not seem able to benefit from this advantage, for instance, Egypt, Laos and the Philippines (measuring PTB) or India (ecological footprint).

I thus conclude that the sign of a country's EUE appears not to be decisive for its trajectory, at least not in and of itself. Internal factors and world system position are equally, or more, important; development and growth are complicated and complex processes, to state the obvious, and the part played by international exchange may not be the key consideration. The conclusion is similar to the one reached by Paul Baran, as discussed in Chapter 4: it is not the exchange as such but the control over the use of resources, and their returns, which determines the outcome.

Put simply, there are many factors at play here. This understanding of the relative importance of EUE is not what we found in the early formulations of the significance of unequal exchange: as we have seen repeatedly, unequal exchange has been held to be the "elementary transfer mechanism" (Emmanuel 1972), securing a "hidden transfer of value from the periphery to the center" (Amin 1976), the explanation of why some countries are "underdeveloped" (Bunker 1985).

There is another objection to this understanding of the importance of EUE which needs to be considered here. I have postulated – in Chapter 2 – that the growing weight of land areas and land-based resources in the global socio-ecological metabolism will keep the prices of primary commodities up, and it would only be natural to expect that they could become a blessing for the countries that harbour them in abundance, thus turning the implication of unequal exchange upside down. From now on, it would be reasonable to expect land areas and land-based resources to benefit the resource-rich economies, be they of the North or the South. The curse of resources could be turned into a blessing.

Such a presumption, however, disregards the fact that economies are not defined by their resource assets alone, not even mainly, but more importantly by their historic position in the global system. Hence, treasured land-based resources may constitute less of a blessing and more of a curse to countries of the South, while countries of the North will thrive from similar resource abundance. Compare Norway and Nigeria, Canada and Congo, Australia and Sudan. The "curse of resources" – a strong belief among mainstream economists as well as in the public opinion – should be reinterpreted in recognition that resources will affect country trajectories differently depending on the world system position of each country.

This is evidenced in Table 6.7, which lists the major exporters of agricultural products. On the one hand, we find that large countries figure prominently, something which is to be expected when it comes to land-based resources such as these. On the other hand, the dominant countries belong to the North as well as to the South.

*Table 6.7* Top ten global exporters of key agricultural products, 2001–2003 (average exported tons)

| Country/region | Percentage of world exports |
| --- | --- |
| USA | Cereals 31, oilseeds 41, meat 19, fibres 27 |
| EU 15 | Cereals 22, oilseeds 8, meat 40, fibres 9, sugar 20 |
| Argentina | Cereals 8, oilseeds 9 |
| Australia | Cereals 7, meat 7, fibres 17, sugar 6 |
| Canada | Cereals 7, oilseeds 7, meat 5 |
| Brazil | Oilseeds 20, meat 9, sugar 6 |
| Uzbekistan | Fibres 9 |
| Thailand | Sugar 10 |
| Cuba | Sugar 7 |
| Bangladesh | Fibres 4 |

Source: FAO 2004, Table 3.

In fact, some of the world's most successful economies (in terms of growth and wealth) are to a surprisingly high degree also leading producers and export-ers of primary commodities. If my hypothesis regarding the crucial role of land in the global socio-ecological metabolism is correct, these are the states which may gain power and influence as the centrality of land-based resources reaffirms itself.

But here we must remind ourselves of a point made in Chapter 4: ecologically unequal exchange takes place as much within as among countries. Behind the veil of nations and countries we find corporations, and we should not confound one with the other: 60 per cent of the global cereals stocks are in private hands, while six private companies account for 80 per cent of the global trade in wheat and rice (McMichael 2009a:287).

Thus, what the growing importance of land areas and land-based resources will entail in terms of social development and the improvement of living con-ditions is not a foregone conclusion; it is closely related to the political alliances and compromises entered into by the various stakeholders. Thus, the question whether land-based resources are a curse or a blessing remains open.

# Part III

# Environmental load displacements

In Part I, I postulated the return of land areas and land-based resources to the centre of the global socio-ecological metabolic regime, based on the constraints which achieving climate stability imposes: no additional deforestation, and no replacement of oil by fossil fuels, conventional or not.

Part II then gauged trade in (mostly embodied) ecological resources and found a pattern which conforms to the theory of ecologically unequal exchange, albeit with exceptions.

This leads me to Part III and a more general argument regarding the appropriation of ecological space by the Centre. Just as the global socio-ecological metabolism of today is based on securing a continuous flow of land-based resources to the Centre, it equally needs to assure a counter-flow of waste and pollution to the Periphery. Both outflows and inflows may be understood as instances of environmental load displacement, the subject of the first chapter of Part III.

The actual areas may not be impressive in some of these appropriations, but they nevertheless have in common that land constitutes the coveted resource, or the pre-condition for the sought-after displacement.

Against this background, the concluding chapter discusses the implications of an emerging new agro-regime in terms of the search for fungible land-areas to secure the food, feed, fibres and fuels and the GHG sinks needed for a global socio-ecological metabolism which recognizes the concurrence of peak oil with peak soil and the need to reach climate stability.

Power relations being what they are, it is not far-fetched to believe that such a new agro-regime will lead to an even greater effort by the Centre to appropriate ecological space, thus again making conflicts over land-based resources the focal point of geopolitically driven land struggles.

# 7 Obvious and obscure displacements

Environmental load displacements, ELD, take two forms, one easy to observe, one more obscured. I will deal with the obscure form of ELD, the transfer of polluting industries to the South, later on in this chapter, but I start out with the obvious and heavily criticized form of ELD, the trade in toxic waste from North to South, a phenomenon which is on the increase in spite of the international regulations which have been set in place to restrict it.

## The obvious displacement: trade and trafficking in waste

Readers unfamiliar with economists' efficiency reasoning may be surprised to learn that traditional economics actually welcomes ELD. In a leaked memo, the then chief economist at the World Bank, Lawrence Summers, maintained that "impeccable ... economic logic" told him that trade in waste from rich to poor countries would increase the efficiency of the global economy, and hence that environmental load displacement ought to be encouraged: "a given amount of health impairing pollution should be done in the country with the lowest cost, which will be the country with the lowest wages" (Summers 1991). Although the memo instantly made Summers notorious, his career did not suffer. After leaving the World Bank he was appointed secretary of the treasury under President Clinton, and subsequently became chairman of the board of Harvard University; he is now chief economic advisor to President Obama.

Summers approves of an already established practice of dumping waste on poor and marginalized peoples, also within the countries of the North, such as the depositing of toxic and nuclear waste on land areas primarily inhabited by indigenous or minority populations (see Martínez-Alier 2002:168–194 for illustrative cases from the USA and South Africa). No wonder, then, that Summers's argument is seen as "canonical" (Martínez-Alier 2002:194) for the environmental justice movement: it is representative of mainstream economics, and less well-known economists advocate an "efficient" distribution of environmental loads in a logic which is no different from Summers's. For instance, a comprehensive survey of the literature on environmental load displacement advises against "an economically inefficient level of pollution" (Brunnermeier and Levinson 2004:1), and poor countries are actually told to accept being "pollution havens" in order to stimulate their own development, pushing Summers's argument to the extreme. As we are informed in a naked apology for environmental load displacement and appropriation of ecological space by the North:

> We must also be aware that LDCs [less developed countries] may have a greater social tolerance and greater absorptive capacity for pollution which can be considered a legitimate source of comparative advantage and lead to the conclusion that the relocation of dirty production to LDCs is "good" for the country in question.
>
> (Cole *et al.* 2008:539)

The underlying argument is that pollution does not have to be sustained forever; once growth takes off, it can "fortunately" be mitigated, as the South will then become more environmentally conscious and impose more environmentally-friendly regulations and taxes, just as the North has done. The problem, it is claimed, is "transient" (Mani and Wheeler 1998:244), "small" (Copeland and Taylor 2004:67) or, according to the World Bank, "not trivial but also not dominant" (World Bank 2008:30). Economists such as these refuse to study what is, and prefer to focus on what might be. From this perspective, environmental load displacement, although real, is a small, passing phenomenon which needs no serious policy intervention of any kind: it will go away by itself. In the meantime, "efficiency" requires that waste and pollution should hit societies and peoples according to their respective "capacities" for dealing with them. Since this capacity to accommodate pollution is assumed to be greater in the global South than in the global North, this is also where the waste ought to go.

But the economists do not appear to realize that they are only proposing a temporary solution: once today's pollution havens refuse to receive their waste, as they are supposed to do as they grow richer, where should we dispose of it? Only by assuming a constantly expanding waste frontier, reaching ever further out into the global system, does this argument make sense. Thus, the logical end point on which the economists' argument is premised is accessing outer space for future ELD.

However, the logic in favour of ELD is not limited to economists, alas, but is also accepted by the Organization for Economic Cooperation and Development (OECD), which welcomes the fact that countries let themselves be used as "pollution havens" for resource and energy-intensive production as part of efficiency-enhancing "trends in the international specialisation in production and relative comparative advantages of different countries" (OECD 2011:20). The wording is reminiscent of Ricardo's trade theory (see Chapter 4), but here "comparative advantage" points a country in the direction of specializing in being a receptacle for the surplus waste of the rich world.

One early expressions of this transfer of environmental loads is the export of pesticides from the Centre to the Periphery, both for use and to be dumped. By the mid-1990s, the United Nations Food and Agriculture Organization assessed that stockpiles of this kind of waste in non-OECD countries were exceeding 100,000 tons; by 2001 the estimates had quintupled (without taking contaminated soil and water into account). Some of the most well-known producers and exporters are transnational chemical giants, for instance American Cyanamid/ BASF, Bayer, Dow, Dupont, and Monsanto (Rosenfeld and Feng 2011:172).

Such transfers are clear cases of the appropriation of ecological space, replicating a pattern which already was traditional in the Centre itself: it is on the poor that the waste is dumped. In this tradition, the Dell computer company contracted the US federal prison industries, UNICOR, to supply prison inmates to do the dismantling of its electronic waste. The purpose was evidently to avoid being criticized for dumping waste on poor people, at home or abroad. But US prisoners felt exploited and remonstrated about their low wages (US$0.20–1.26 per hour at Atwater prison) and unhealthy working conditions. As one inmate said: "Funny, isn't it, how this stuff is unsafe for public dumps, but not for us lowly prison inmates?!?" (Pellow 2007:206–212). The Dell case shows that getting rid of toxic waste is no easy matter. Corporations and governments which have tried to go along with Summers's "impeccable" logic and dump their waste in the Periphery, have found that they clash head-on with environmental consciousness globally, not only where the dump is located.

One of the most notorious cases occurred in 1986 when the city of Philadelphia rented *Khian Sea*, a ship registered in Liberia, to get rid of 15,000 tons of its incinerator ash. The *Khian Sea* left on an odyssey that was to last 27 months, attempting to offload its dirty cargo in various continents, passing the Bahamas, the Dominican Republic, Honduras, Puerto Rico, Bermuda, the Netherlands Antilles, Haiti (where it illegally disposed of 3,700 tons), Senegal, Guinea-Bissau, Cape Verde, Sri Lanka, Indonesia and the Philippines. Everywhere, the ship was turned away, until it finally "lost" its cargo somewhere in the Indian Ocean (Pellow 2007:107–116, Rosenfeld and Feng 2011:171).

The logic here is clear: the rich, white North is trying to dump its waste on lands where poor, non-white people live. To use my terminology: the US is appropriating ecological space outside of its own borders. But what may not be immediately evident is that the North (in this case, the city of Philadelphia) had put itself in a position where it needed to secure such ecological space by being forced, first, to close down its own dumps and replace them with incinerators, and, subsequently, to dismantle the incinerators as public protests against them picked up. The waste simply had to be displaced somewhere outside of the US. The practice continuous today as witnessed by shipbreaking and trade in e-waste (the following is culled from NGO Shipbreaking Platform 2007; BAN 2011; GAO 2008; ETBC 2012; World Bank 2010).

After World War II, the USA, UK and Japan were the main shipbreaking nations, but in the 1960s shipbreaking moved south, first to Southern Europe, later to Asia, starting in South Korea and Taiwan, then continuing to China, India, Pakistan, Bangladesh, the Philippines and Vietnam. Just from these facts, we can conclude that shipbreaking constitutes a case of environmental load displacement: what was formerly dismantled in the North has been passed on to the South.

The ideal sites for shipbreaking are shores with gently sloping beaches but with rocky bottoms which allow the ships to be stranded during high tide, thus avoiding expensive dry docks. Today, around 700 to 800 vessels are "beached" in this way each year, half of them at the world's major shipbreaking facilities at Alang-Sosiya, Gujarat, northwestern India, an average of one vessel a day: see Figure 7.1.

The workers engaged in this business are super-exploited: high rates of accidents, exposure to dangerous and poisonous substances – cadmium, chromium, lead, mercury, asbestos, PCB, oil, flame retardants, radioactive materials are found on the contaminated beaches and in the lungs of the workers – lack of personal protection equipment, weak or absent trade unions.

In India, shipbreaking is six to seven times more deadly than mining, the second most life-threatening industry in India in terms of its death toll: the rate of fatal accidents in the Indian shipbreaking industry is 2 per 1,000 workers compared to 0.3 per 1,000 in mining (Demaria 2010:255). And in Bangladesh, one-quarter of the workforce on the shipbreaking yards are children (Rosenfeld and Feng 2011:173).

A case which attracted widespread attention is the dismantling of the cruiser *SS Norway*, which was directed by its owners to Bangladesh for breaking. This vessel – once one of the world's largest cruisers, second only to *Queen Elizabeth II* and the *Titanic*, originally under the name *SS France* – contained significant volumes of toxic materials, such as 900 tons of asbestos and PCB, and its decontamination was estimated to cost at least €17 million; the scrap value amounted

*Figure 7.1* Shipbreaking, Alang-Sosiya, India, 2009 (source: www.googleearth.com, accessed 2 February 2012; Google and the Google logo are registered trademarks of Google Inc., used with permission).

to only €10 million. Hence, "cleaning up" prior to export was seen as uneconomical by the Norwegian owners. The breaking up of the ship was refused by the Bangladeshi government before the owners turned to India and sailed for Alang-Sosiya (Moen 2008:1058).

Also in India, the breaking up of the vessel – now re-named *SS Blue Lady* – was contested on the grounds that its export from Norway to India violated the OECD Polluter Pays Principle, as well as the Basel Convention rules on controlling transboundary movements of hazardous waste and the Ban agreement on prior decontamination of waste, all of which Norway is committed to abide by. The case was finally settled in 2007 by the Indian Supreme Court, which allowed the breaking of the vessel based on an argument which pitted the environment and the interest of a minority against the economy and the interest of the majority. In its ruling, the Supreme Court held:

> It cannot be disputed that no development is possible without some adverse effect on the ecology and the environment.... A balance has to be struck between the two interests. Where the commercial venture of enterprise would bring in results which are far more useful for the people, difficulty of a small number of people has to be bypassed. The comparative hardships have to be balanced and the convenience and benefit to a larger section of the people has to get primacy over comparatively lesser hardships.
>
> (quoted in Demaria 2010:258–259)

With the principle of balancing opposed effects – benefits against costs, the majority against the minority – the Indian Supreme Court legitimized environmental load displacement and the appropriation of Indian land (and labour) as part of ELD from the Centre to the Periphery; simultaneously, the court disregarded a number of international legal obligations of both the sending and the receiving countries.

The transfer of electronic waste is another example of ELD, allegedly for re-conditioning and re-use. The major importing countries, whose lands and labour forces are appropriated and exploited, are China, Mexico, India and Nigeria. Nigeria is reported to receive 500 containers a week with used computers from Europe and North America.

Just as in the case of shipbreaking, agents take temporary ownership of the waste and then resell it to corporations in countries where the dumping grounds are located. The origin of the waste being dumped is sometimes somewhat ironic: a considerable share comes from "recycling" or from gifts of second-hand equipment, collected in order to bridge the "digital divide"; however, 50 to 80 per cent of e-waste collected in the US is not recycled at all, but simply disposed of in the importing country after being smashed and burned; only a small share of the waste – mostly costly metals – is recycled in one form or the other.

An example of this kind of environmental load displacement is the exporting of television sets and monitors (of the old, bulky kind), which contain lead, dioxins, cadmium, barium, beryllium, mercury, and obnoxious gases of various kinds, all of which are released as the tubes are burned by workers, often children, who lack adequate protective equipment. As a consequence, children and adults living in the world's major e-waste "processing" region, Guiyu in China, have unusually high levels of lead and fire retardants in their blood, a not unexpected outcome of adhering to the "impeccable logic" of Lawrence Summers, and of using China's "comparative advantage" according to the OECD.

## The obscure displacement: pollution havens

A more hidden appropriation of ecological space takes the shape of outsourcing of pollution- and energy-intensive industries from the North to the South, either through foreign direct investments (FDIs), or as plain sourcing of the produce from locally owned facilities. Both routes lead to a flow of finished products and goods from South to North, something which for the last 35 years has been known as the new international division of labour (Fröbel *et al.* 1977, Warren 1980).

But while it has been recognized that the global industrial production shifted geographical location – leading to the emergence of a limited number of newly industrializing countries, NICs – it has largely gone unnoticed that the two flows are connected: the flow of finished products from the South to the North returns as waste. It becomes more and more of a recursive process, where outsourcing to the South leads to imports of embedded ecological space to the North, which subsequently returns to the South, as we have seen, as waste, continuing the process of appropriation of ecological space.

In recent years, a large body of studies has been published substantiating this kind of ELD: foreign investments from, and exports to, the North bring environmental exploitation and degradation to the South. In economists' terms, the North manages to "externalize" – or cost shift, to use a phrase coined by Joan Martínez-Alier (Martínez-Alier 2002:30) – its consumption footprint to poor countries, either through trade or through FDIs. Table 7.1 sums up the evidence.

The more foreign corporations invest in the South and the more economies of the South export to the North, the worse the ecological status in the South becomes: pesticide and fertilizer use as well as deforestation increase, biological diversity deteriorates, $CO_2$ emissions grow, water pollution and noxious gas emissions rise. The relationships hold for both drivers, FDIs North → South as well as exports South → North, and for both the primary and the secondary sectors.

## Land grabbing

I argue that the distinction between strategic and non-strategic land-based resources is becoming less relevant, as we may expect ever more conflicts over fungible land-based resources. Put differently: all land-based resources are strategic now; the simultaneous increase in demand for food, feed, fibres and fuels spells competition for limited land areas.

*Table 7.1* Appropriated ecological space in the South

| Period | Deteriorating environmental status in the South as measured by | Sector | Driver |
|--------|---------------------------------------------------------------|--------|--------|
| 1990–2000 | Pesticide and fertilizer use | Primary | FDI North → South |
| 1990–2005 | Deforestation | Primary | FDI North → South |
| 1970–2000 | Deforestation | Primary | Exports South → North |
| 2005 | Threatened mammals | Primary | Exports South → North |
| 1975–2000 | $CO_2$ emissions | Manufacture | FDI North → South |
| 1960–2005 | $CO_2$ emissions | Exports | Exports South → North |
| 1975–2000 | Water pollution | Manufacture | FDI North → South |
| 1990–2000 | Noxious gas emissions | Manufacture | FDI North → South |

Sources: Jorgenson 2007, 2008, 2009, 2012, Jorgenson *et al.* 2007, 2009, Jorgenson and Kuykendall 2008, Shandra *et al.* 2009.

Note
The dependent variables all deal with absolute levels of pollution or resource exhaustion in the South.

It is in this light that I see the swiftly growing business activity which has swept Africa, Asia and Latin America, with some incursions into Eastern Europe, beginning in the first decade of the twenty-first century: the appropriation of land for commercial purposes. The deals have grown from modest levels – approximately one million hectares – at the outset of the decade to covering more than ten millions hectares annually more recently. The branding of such land deals is a controversial issue: some, including the World Bank, prefer "investments" or "acquisitions", while others would consider anything but "land grab" or even "theft" a euphemism, for instance non-governmental organizations such as GRAIN and peasant organizations such as Via Campesina. Reinforcing this perspective of illicit land acquisitions is the fact that investments in land, according to an International Monetary Fund study, appears to be closely related to poor governance in the countries where the grabs take place: in contrast to other FDIs, land deals are attracted to "countries where governance of the land sector and tenure security are weak" (Arezki *et al.* 2011:4).

Irrespective of what term one prefers, however, observers agree that there has been a new rush into controlling land, and with the land the water resources needed, and sometimes the labour to make both of them profitable. After decades of being seen as a commodity of little commercial interest, land is today increasingly of central concern to any actor considering food security, climate stability, or energy politics in general, a situation which is similar to the colonial preoccupation with land and land-based resources.

### The framing of land grabbing

Land grabs were originally framed in relation to rising food prices, and they were defined by three traits:

- the deals were large, over 1,000 hectares;
- the grabbers, corporations as well as states, were based outside the territories where the grabs took place; and
- the purpose of the grabs was to supply the international market, or the home market of the investor, with food.

That this pattern is reminiscent of the earlier colonial period of land grabs has been noted: "Foreign private corporations getting new forms of control over farmland to produce food not for the local communities but for someone else. Did someone say colonialism was a thing of the past?" (GRAIN 2008:3). However, by now it has become clear that this definition of land grabbing is too limited and does not grasp the scale of the phenomenon, nor the actors involved. One weakness is the dependence on the size of the grab, with the arbitrary limit set at 1,000 ha: why should a 300 ha vine orchard signify less of a grab than 100,000 ha of eucalyptus plantation, or 500,000 ha of grazing land? Different areas may in fact have similar significance in terms of capital needed to secure the land, and in terms of the economic gains which can be reaped from a given investment (Borras *et al.* 2012:850).

Furthermore, the emphasis on the nationality of the grabbers as well as the focus on deals to secure food run the risk of failing to see who the actual investors are, and why they acquire land: there is a *general* interest in land and land-based resources, for various purposes, from food to speculation via agrofuels and feed production. At the same time, the grabbers are to be found everywhere, in the private and public sectors, and they are based in poor as well as in rich countries.

In fact, a combination of drivers is aiming at land in order to meet the global demand for food, feed, fibres and fuels, and any attempt to focus only on one driver, or one kind of grabber, or one region being grabbed, will reduce the larger significance of land-based resources, of which land grabbing is just one symptom (Borras *et al.* 2011: 9).

Geopolitical concerns, as I noted in Chapter 2, play a role in pushing for more land grabs, especially the export bans imposed by some exporting countries in order to prevent food riots and improve the local availability of food in the face of the rising prices of 2008. Violent protests have spread – the list is long: manifestations have been reported from Burkina Faso, Cameroon, Côte d'Ivoire, Egypt, Guinea, Haiti, Honduras, Indonesia, Kenya, Malaysia, Mauritania, Morocco, Mozambique, Pakistan, Russia, Senegal, Thailand, Tunisia, and Yemen (Cohen and Garrett 2009). Many countries took preventive measures and reduced their agricultural exports, among them Argentina, Bangladesh, Bolivia, Burkina Faso, Cambodia, China, Egypt, Ethiopia, Guinea, Haiti, Honduras,

India, Madagascar, Malawi, Russia, Uganda, Ukraine and Zambia (FAO 2009b:54–57, IATP 2012:33). As a follow-up on this experience, many import-dependent countries are now increasing their stocks of food as a precautionary step (see Box 7.1), and some of them are also stepping up their investments in land overseas.

---

**Box 7.1  Building food reserves around the world**

A number of countries are increasing their stocks or otherwise changing their policies to protect their home markets from expected disturbance from the global markets.

**Middle East**: Saudi Arabia and Egypt are aiming at a six months' supply of wheat, while Iraq is opting for as much as a full year's consumption. In addition, United Arab Emirates, Qatar and Jordan are boosting their storage capacities.

**Sub-Saharan Africa**: Kenya is doubling its reserves, and Ethiopia is considering increasing them as well, while Nigeria has adopted a policy of keeping 15 per cent of its needs in stock, quite limited compared to other countries. Similarly, Sudan is keeping only a small reserve.

**South Asia**: Bangladesh is increasing its stocks of wheat and rice after having reduced them in the 1990s following advice to depend on the market. On the other hand, Pakistan and India have enjoyed bumper harvests of rice as well as wheat, and may consider increasing their exports.

**East Asia and Southeast Asia**: China has, at least hitherto, embraced a policy of 95 per cent self-sufficiency, save for a major dependency on soy imports. South Korea, Indonesia and the Philippines are all trying to increase their reserves of rice.

Source: IATP 2012:33–35

---

## Land grabbing 2000–2010

Assessments of the total land areas acquired vary, with 227 million hectares the highest reported for the period 2001–2010 (Oxfam 2011b:2). However, some deals are never carried through, some projects never implemented, some investments falsely reported, etc. Table 7.2 uses verified cases of land grabbing to show that at least 71 million hectares (including in Eastern Europe) were grabbed in the period 2000–2010. This is indeed impressive, larger than the total area of Sweden (48.5 million hectares), Germany (35.7 Mha), France (54.9 Mha), or the United Kingdom (24.3 Mha).

Investments in agrofuel feedstocks dominate the overall picture, followed by food and forestry. All in all, these three commodities account for almost 90 per cent of the verified grabs, with the following distribution: feedstocks for agrofuels 58 per cent, food 18 per cent, and forestry 13 per cent.

*Table 7.2* Verified land grabs, 2000–2010 (million hectares)

| Land acquired in | Origin of investors (%) | Commodities (%) | Total land area (Mha) |
|---|---|---|---|
| Africa | Asia 39<br>Africa 20<br>Europe 19 | Agrofuels 66<br>Food 15<br>Forestry 7<br>Tourism 9 | 34 |
| Asia | Asia 89<br>Middle East 6<br>Europe 3 | Agrofuels 56<br>Food 15<br>Forestry 20<br>Industry 6 | 29 |
| Latin America | Latin America 37<br>North America 35<br>Asia 13 | Agrofuels 33<br>Food 27<br>Minerals, oil 24<br>Forestry 10 | 6 |

Source: Based on Anseeuw *et al.* 2012, Figures 3–6.

Note
Verified grabs = reported and cross-referenced land deals.

The geographical pattern is clear. Most grabs have taken place in Africa, approximately half: 34 million out of 71 million hectares.

The sizes of the areas of the land deals vary considerably. According to a survey performed by the World Bank, areas vary from a surprisingly small 700 hectares in Ethiopia to an amazingly large 59,000 hectares in Liberia (World Bank 2011:62). This makes one of the most noted land grabs (although never realized) an exception: in 2008, the South Korean conglomerate Daewoo signed a contract with Madagascar for a 99-year lease on 1.3 Mha, possibly contributing to the subsequent downfall of the government in 2009 (*Financial Times* 2009). But although this aborted deal was exceptional, it is not unique. The Chinese government is reported to have grabbed 2.8 Mha in the Democratic Republic of Congo for palm oil production, while the British bioenergy corporation Global Green Energy controls 900,000 hectares for agrofuels in Mali, Guinea, and Senegal (Oakland Institute 2011). Similarly, Pro Savana, a joint venture involving Brazilian and Japanese actors, has obtained 8 Mha in Mozambique on a 50 years' lease, mostly along the Nacala corridor, to mix Brazilian agricultural know-how with Japanese funding. The reason is simple, explains the owner of Brazilian cotton plantations in the fertile Mato Grosso state, also one of the sugarcane states of Brazil:

Mozambique is a Mato Grosso in the middle of Africa, with free land, without environmental impediments, and with much cheaper freight to China. Today, in addition to land being exceedingly expensive in Mato Grosso, it's impossible to get a license to deforest and clean an area.

(Augustin 2012)

It has been noted that some of the most important investors globally (in area terms) come from Asia, and they are both states and corporations. Large investors in this group include India, China, South Korea, Saudi Arabia and United Arab Emirates, and these investors frequently figure prominently in the list of the major culprits driving the global land grab, though the pattern is more complex; see Figure 7.2.

Figure 7.2 shows a wide range of grabbers, including the fast-growing economies of the world, but also with a fair number of not-so-often-talked-about grabbers, from the largest of them all, India, to the smallest of the 20 grabbers which qualify for inclusion here, Sweden. Also note that the USA appears as a significant grabber, outdoing China, a role which frequently goes missing in other accounts. Of course, were we to measure land grabbing per capita of the grabbing country, the hierarchy of grabbers would look quite different, and Sweden would appear among the major ones.

However, attributing a nationality to the land grabbers runs the risk of obfuscating the complex character of land deals. Sweden and the USA, as well as South Korea, Saudi Arabia and Brazil, just to mention a few of the grabbers, mix private capital and state corporations with international agencies and finance institutions, including pension and development cooperation funds. In the Swedish case, for instance, both a the major public pensions fund – Andra AP

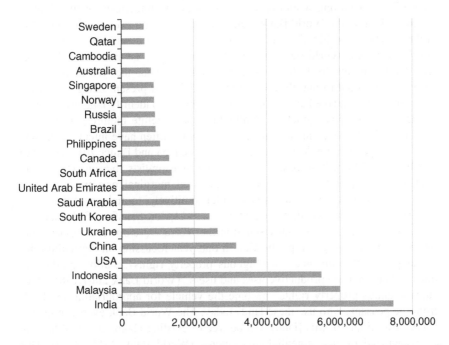

*Figure 7.2* The land grabbers, 2000–2010: areas acquired in hectares, by country of origin of the investors, the cut-off for inclusion in this graph being 200 ha (source: Olsson *et al.* 2012, Figure 6, used with permission).

Fonden – and the public risk capital agency Swedfund, funded by the Swedish aid budget, participate in land grabs: Andra AP Fonden is party to a joint venture with the US pension giant TIAA-CREF (Teachers Insurance and Annuity Association – College Retirement Equities Fund) in Brazil, and Swedfund has joined forces with the Swiss transnational Addax Oryx in appropriating areas for sugarcane ethanol in Sierra Leone.

Add to this transnational corporations such as global food and agribusiness giants Cargill, Archer Daniels Midland, Du Pont, Deere and Monsanto; and add again private and publicly owned oil corporations, from Shell to Brazil's Petrobras, and it soon becomes easier to say who is not involved in land grabbing than who is (Dauvergne and Neville 2010:638–639; Holt-Giménez and Shattuck 2009:183; Borras *et al.* 2010:577–578).

Another new trend is the existence of intermediaries, or facilitators, which make sure that controversial deals are carried through. In southern Africa this role is played by South Africa and its corporations; in Latin America, Brazil and Brazilian firms may front on behalf of other investors; and in Asia, a similar function has been detected for Vietnam and Thailand (Cotula 2012:658–659).

### The empty land argument

The World Bank has entered the game of finding large land areas, the appropriation of which no-one would oppose since they are underused or marginal or abandoned, or so the World Bank maintains. In a scoping exercise, it found 446 million hectares worldwide available for investments in commercial agriculture, mostly in Africa (World Bank 2011). These are very large areas indeed: global crop land amounts to 1,500 million hectares, so what the World Bank has "detected" is equal to one-third of all land which is at present being cultivated. These figures are arrived at by using satellite images to identify land use, thereby conflating land cover, which is identifiable from satellite pictures, with actual land use, which is not; this is a mistake, "as people often have intentions behind land use that cannot be deciphered remotely" (Nalepa and Bauer 2012:410). For instance, 50–200 million pastoralists and agro-pastoralists live on African dry lands which frequently are described as underused, marginal, or empty.

The way to access these areas is, counter-intuitively, to make sure that property rights are distributed, which allows a posterior transfer of the land to resource-rich grabbers. As flatly stated in the *World Development Report 2008*, the World Bank's flagship publication in that year focussing on Agriculture for Development: "Secure and unambiguous property rights ... allow markets to transfer land to more productive uses and users" (World Bank 2007:138). Thus, "unambiguous property rights" become the vehicle for appropriating the lands from the peasants who use these lands today. The World Bank even admits that "very little, if any of this [land] will be free of existing claims that will have to be recognized by any potential investment" (World Bank 2011:78–79). This echoes the conclusion reached by a previous World Bank study which claimed that 90 per cent of West African crop lands are "underused", and that therefore

West Africa was a "sleeping giant", although it inadvertently recognized that fierce land conflicts probably lay ahead if its advice was followed: "Virtually all areas are claimed by some individuals or groups or used in some way" (World Bank 2009:1–2).

Apart from the dubious assumption that there are large areas lying dormant, waiting for investors to awaken them, the empty land argument is disingenuous also in another sense: why would land grabbers opt for such hitherto unused or marginal lands – should they exist – and not prefer more easily accessible, and more profitable, areas? Indeed, studies of *actual* land grabs in Senegal, Mali, Mozambique and Rwanda show unsurprisingly that investors, when they can, go for "the best land in terms of water availability and irrigation potential, soil fertility, proximity to markets or availability of infrastructure" (Cotula 2012:655).

## Concluding remarks

Investing in pollution and energy-intensive production facilities in the South; outsourcing production from the North to the South and then importing the products; and finally returning the produce in the shape of waste to the very same countries from whence they originally came – all are part and parcel of one recursive system, giving a new twist to the global metabolic rift: the resources return as waste, thus adding further stress to an already over-exploited ecological system instead of providing the means by which to renew it.

In this way, environmental load displacement constitutes an important aspect of the appropriation of ecological space, a key trait of today's global socio-ecological metabolism. Not only are land-based resources and primary commodities appropriated by the North; space to dismantle and absorb waste are equally part of this circular flow, just as central as other forms of accessing land-based resources.

It merits underlining, once more, that grabbers active in these appropriations straddle most of the usual divides we are used to: North–South, private–public, financial–productive, large–small. A case in point is a study of the water which land grabbers access through their deals, which I came across as I was finalizing the manuscript of this book: as much as 60 per cent of the water resources grabbed was controlled by stakeholders based in only seven countries: USA, United Arab Emirates, India, United Kingdom, Egypt, China and Israel (Rulli *et al.* 2013). Although this list is only partially the same as the countries included in Figure 7.2, it shows, just as all other summaries of the stakeholders involved, that as land and land-based resources – such as water – have come to the fore globally as well as nationally, land grabbers are to be found everywhere.

# 8 The argument revisited

## The return to the land

The industrial socio-ecological metabolic regime has by now established itself around the globe as the dominant order, and the land areas where the previous agrarian regime still dominates are by comparison of less importance. This industrial regime, evidently, has been based on the availability of fossil fuels, first coal and then oil. But although it is common to describe a metabolic regime by only one dominant feature, this runs the risk of neglecting the considerable overlap that exists from one regime to another: each new metabolic flow does not so much replace as add another layer to the existing set-up.

This holds especially for the rise of oil after World War II. Coal has continued to be important for the global socio-ecological metabolism; its share of the global energy supply in 2009 was approximately the same as in 1973, 27 and 25 per cent respectively. What is more important, the absolute volume of coal has almost tripled: with a growing total energy use – from 6,111 million tons of oil equivalents (Mtoe) in 1973 to 12,150 Mtoe in 2010, an increase of 199 per cent – the coal grew, from 2,235 Mtoe in 1973 to 6,186 Mtoe in 2010 (or by 277 per cent; IEA 2011a). In fact – as I showed in Figure 2.2 – we are living in a socio-ecological metabolic regime driven by oil-coal-gas-nuclear power, not in a regime dominated by oil.

How the future metabolic system will develop is not easy to say, of course, but coal will surely be part of it, in the short term simply because it is available, easily and cheaply. However, coal may not be a long-term solution to the global socio-ecological metabolic needs, as it also may be approaching its own peak level: already by 2020 global energy supply from coal is forecasted to level off, only to start a sharp decline after 2050 (Energy Watch Group 2007). Thus peak oil may soon be followed by peak coal.

Furthermore, both coal and oil have encountered declining levels of energy return on energy invested, EROI, making them less interesting from an energy-efficiency point of view. For instance, the EROI of oil has fallen from over 100:1 in the early stages of oil exploration at the outset of the twentieth century, to today's 18:1 (Hall *et al.* 2009: 35, Murphy and Hall 2011:64). One reason for this decline in EROI is that oil and coal sources are more difficult to access; they are also of inferior quality. This is not accounted for in the recent update by the Organization for Economic Cooperation and Development

(OECD)'s International Energy Agency (IEA), *World Energy Outlook 2012*, which counts on "a surge in unconventional supplies" after 2020, including deep-water oil in Brazil, oil sands in Canada, and shale gas and oil in the USA. Especially optimistic is the IEA forecast for North America, which is presented as a future net exporter of (unconventional) oil, and for the USA, which is expected to be almost self-sufficient in energy terms by 2020 (IEA 2012). But for these unconventional energy sources, the EROI is still lower, probably around 2:1 (Cleveland and O'Connor 2011:283), a fact which goes unnoticed by the IEA.

Land-based energy sources may not be of much help either, at least not if they are to be based on maize, the preferred feedstock in the US mandate. Although estimates of the EROI for maize ethanol vary greatly, none of the assessments has EROI surpassing 2:1 (with low-point estimates actually being less than 1:1, that is, more energy is used in the production process than contained in the fuel; Hall *et al.* 2011:264).

So, adding peak coal and EROI to climate stabilization, we are faced with still more restrictions for the future metabolic regime: now it is squeezed between peak oil, peak coal, peak soil, and declining EROIs all around. This spells, I believe, a stalemate in terms of metabolic regimes: the old industrial regime cannot continue based on fossil fuels, but a new regime cannot be borne unless it resolves the basic issue of finding new sources to satisfy its socio-ecological metabolic needs. This will lead to a conflict over land areas and land-based resources, challenging present land-use patterns. The price rises recorded to date are only the first and probably most pacific of the consequences of this contradiction demand-supply, the surge in land grabbing constituting yet one more indication of where we are heading.

## A hypothetical future: substituting land areas for fossil fuels

Nowhere is the conflict over land more pronounced than when it comes to assessing the possibility of substituting fossil fuels with land-based energy sources. We have already come across this in Chapter 2, where various estimates of feedstock areas were presented to replace oil for petrol use. Here, I will look at the overall use of fossil fuels and speculate what would happen to land use if fossil fuels were to be replaced by agrofuels. In order to reach a conservative figure of needed areas, I shall use Brazilian sugarcane area-efficiency, the highest in the world.

The procedure is not new: 50 years ago biologist Georg Borgström calculated the areas needed to produce a rich country's imports of food and fish. Borgström called such appropriated space "ghost acres" and concluded that if every human on Earth lived as the average Dutch, another planet would be needed (Borgström 1964:233). The conclusion is similar to the one reached in Chapter 4, comparing the global ecological footprint with the bio-productive land and sea areas.

I will proceed in two steps. First, I ask how large land areas would be needed in order for economies to become independent of fossil fuel *imports*; second, I bring the example to its logical conclusion and estimate the land areas required to replace *all* fossil fuels and nuclear power.

If the OECD were to replace its net fossil fuel imports by best-case Brazilian ethanol, 477 million hectares would be needed, approximately one-third of today's global crop land: see Table 8.1.

Where and how could such land areas be appropriated? Most likely by deforestation, either directly or indirectly. Directly, it is already taking place in Indonesia and Malaysia, for instance, to make room for the production of palm oil; indirectly, as in the Brazilian case, deforestation occurs first in the Cerrado, and then in the Amazon at the end of the chain of events unleashed by the expansion of sugarcane cultivation over crop lands and pastures. Thus, if we intend to replace fossil fuels by agrofuels in order to reduce climate gases, we are likely to replace one source of greenhouse gases (GHG) by another: land-use change and deforestation for fossil fuels.

On the other hand, if the motive for reducing the dependence on fossil fuels is geopolitical, we need not be concerned with the ecological consequences, but the boosting of agrofuels would still be problematic since we would exchange the dependency on oil-producing countries for a reliance on land-rich countries, primarily in South America, Eastern Europe and southeast Asia; this second option may be as problematic as the present situation from the point of view of secure and uninterrupted flows from Periphery to Centre.

I now take this scenario one step further by asking how much land area would be needed to substitute *all* fossil energy with agrofuels. Again, the estimates are conservative as I am using Brazilian land area efficiency figures; see Table 8.2.

*Table 8.1* Net imports of fossil fuel and the land areas needed to replace it, 2007

| | Net imports of fossil fuel in Mtoe[a] | → equals TJ[b] | → equals Mtons sugarcane[c] | → equals Mha sugarcane[d] |
|---|---|---|---|---|
| OECD | 1,821 Mtoe | $7,624 \times 10^4$ | 38,120 Mtons | 477 Mha |
| Brazil | 25 Mtoe | $105 \times 10^4$ | 525 Mtons | 7 Mha |
| China | 167 Mtoe | $699 \times 10^4$ | 3,495 Mtons | 44 Mha |
| Germany | 202 Mtoe | $846 \times 10^4$ | 4,230 Mtons | 53 Mha |
| India | 150 Mtoe | $628 \times 10^4$ | 3,140 Mtons | 39 Mha |
| Japan | 435 Mtoe | $1,821 \times 10^4$ | 9,105 Mtons | 114 Mha |
| USA | 714 Mtoe | $2,989 \times 10^4$ | 14,945 Mtons | 187 Mha |

Notes

a A small share of electricity imports are included in the figures for the US, Brazil and India. 1 Mtoe = $4.1868 \times 10^4$ TJ. Source: IEA 2009.

b TJ = $10^{12}$ joule. Source: IEA 2009.

c Energy content 2000 MJ/ton sugarcane. I have not deducted the energy used to produce ethanol, as it is of the same magnitude as the energy content of the by-products from ethanol production (bagasse and electricity generation): the inputs are estimated to contain 234 MJ/ton of sugarcane, while the co-generated products are 259 MJ/ton. Source: BNDES and CGEE 2008, Table 12.

d Highest average Brazilian sugarcane yield assumed: 80 t of sugarcane/ha. Source: BNDES and CGEE 2008, Table 7.

*Table 8.2* Total use of fossil and nuclear energy and the land areas needed to replace it, 2007

| | TPES of fossil fuel and nuclear energy in Mtoe | → equals TJ | → equals Mtons sugarcane | → equals Mha sugarcane |
|---|---|---|---|---|
| OECD | 5,119 | $21,432 \times 10^4$ | 107,161 | 1,340 |
| Non-OECD | 5,386 | $22,550 \times 10^4$ | 112,751 | 1,409 |
| World | 10,505 | $43,982 \times 10^4$ | 219,912 | 2,749 |

See Notes at Table 8.1.

The required land areas are not small: for the world as a whole we would need 2,749 million hectares, or 180 per cent of today's cropped land area. As a complete replacement of fossil fuels would require close to twice the present global crop areas in the best of cases, we would have to look for land areas for food, feed and fibres elsewhere. Of course, if we entertain more realistic scenarios, with lower area productivity than in Brazil, the areas needed to replace fossil fuels will be concomitantly larger, and the contradictions among the competing land uses still fiercer.

## A sequence of cumulative agro-regimes

Over the years, the role of land areas and land-based resources in the global socio-ecological metabolism has shifted. Sociologists Harriet Friedmann and Philip McMichael have described this shift in terms of a series of "food regimes" (Friedmann and McMichael 1989; McMichael 2009b), but I believe that "agro-regimes" is a more appropriate concept to the study of the use of land areas. The fact that land is "fungible", that land can be used for many purposes, gives the simultaneous increase in the quest for land for food, feed, fibres and fuels its significance, and explains why an expansion of agrofuels cannot but enter into direct conflict with other land uses (since I postulate that no new land may be cleared for agriculture).

I will restrict my discussion to the period after World War II, but even with this limited historical perspective we find three regimes. Each regime is characterized by its unique mixture of arena, driver, legitimating ideology, and emblematic product: see Table 8.3.

Agro-regimes have evolved from being basically a vehicle for producing food, via incorporating feed for the food and meat industry, to also providing the feedstocks for fuels. But the sequence is not one of replacement but rather of accumulation, just as we found in relation to the use of the various energy sources to fuel our socio-ecological metabolism.

But irrespective of this cumulative process, the regimes are different and some trends are clear: the regimes have gradually migrated from the national via

*Table 8.3* Three agro-regimes since 1945

| Agro-regime | Main arena | Main driver | Legitimation | Emblematic product |
|---|---|---|---|---|
| Food | National | States | National self-reliance | Wheat |
| Feed | International | States and corporations | Market efficiency | Soybean, meat |
| Fuel | Global | States, corporations and finance capital | Climate change | Ethanol, biodiesel |

the international to the global arena, integrating new drivers – corporations for the feed regime, finance capital for the fuel regime – and benefiting from new justifications and legitimations.

The dominating logic of the first regime, the agro-food regime, was to achieve self-sufficiency of food in order – at least as a legitimation – to hedge against a possible return to the 1914–1945 years of blockade and the resulting rationing of food. This objective was so strong that it kept agriculture as a whole outside the General Agreement on Tariffs and Trade, GATT, established in 1947. Another important sector which also was excluded from GATT was textiles, supposedly here as well to secure the continuous supply of an essential good.

But although the purpose may have been to protect national food markets, the combination of state protection with high degrees of subsidies to the agricultural sector of the North created large surpluses which were channelled to the countries of the South, where they were either dumped to out-compete local food production, and thus create future markets for food exports from the North, or shipped as food aid (which had a similar negative impact on local self-reliance). This agro-food regime thus was tailored to the needs of the North, post-World War II. In terms of ecological exchange, however, we here have a situation where the North is exporting more embodied areas than it is importing, which testifies to the different logic of the agro-food regime as compared to the present agrofuel regime where the reverse flow from South to North is dominant.

The second regime, the agro-feed regime, witnessed the increase of feedstocks for meat production and for the food industry, mixing old and new agricultural superpowers (see Table 6.7 for a representative list). The agro-feed regime brought forth new agricultural exporters, creatively dubbed new agricultural countries, NACs, by Harriet Friedmann (Friedmann 1993:45–47). This change went largely unnoticed compared to the attention afforded the parallel shift in industrial production in the newly industrializing countries, but the fact is that the NACs became essential to the global socio-ecological metabolism as providers of feed for the meat industry, and as suppliers of vegetables, fruits, citrus and cut flowers to the North. Thus, the agro-feed regime saw three flows of land-based resources: food from the traditional large exporting countries, the settler colonies of old, primarily the US, Canada, Australia, and Argentina;

simultaneously, new flows of feed from Argentina, Brazil, Canada and the US for the global food and meat industry; and, again concomitantly, a flow of high-priced fruits and vegetables from the South to the affluent markets of the North, especially its urban centres. Kenya is here a case in point: it is today one of the world's leading exporters of cut flowers.

In this agro-feed regime, not only food but equally feed are produced and transported around the globe, sharpening the substitutability of, and thus the competition for, fungible land areas and land-based resources. To this we must now add the most recent regime, the agrofuel phase, where agrofuels are joining the already long list of essential commodities to the global socio-ecological metabolism.

Viewing agriculture as embedded in a series of cumulative regimes in this way sheds new light on one of the more confusing aspects of the World Trade Organization, WTO, which replaced GATT in 1995. What needs explaining is why agriculture was included in the WTO after having remained outside of the GATT for almost 50 years. The conventional understanding is that neither the US nor the EU had any intention of actually opening up their agricultural sectors to competition; they only used agriculture as a negotiation tactic to get countries such as India and Brazil to accept other agreements – especially patent rights – which the countries of the South would agree to only if they were "paid off" by an agreement on agriculture (UNDP 2003 provides a summary of the negotiations and the establishment of the WTO in this light). The tactics worked well, and the new WTO did include an Agreement on Agriculture as well as an Agreement on Trade Related Aspects of Intellectual Property Rights, TRIPS, which catered to the interests of the patent-holding corporations of the North.

The fact that the US and the EU have, since the establishment of the WTO, failed to fulfil their obligations according to the agreement on agriculture has been seen as a confirmation of this interpretation: the EU and the US had never intended to give up supporting and protecting their agricultural sectors, the agreement on agriculture being a scam to get other agreements through the negotiations. For instance, the average tariff protection for agricultural products was still 4 percentage points higher than for industrial goods in 2010, a gap which has remained stable since WTO was launched in 1995 (Datt *et al.* 2011:4); this indicates the same greater willingness to protect agriculture compared to industry.

This interpretation, although popular, is not exhaustive, as it disregards the fact that the agro-food regime had passed into a new phase at about the time the WTO negotiations were initiated in 1986: the national logic of the agro-food regime was no longer dominant, as the need of the agro-feed regime for an open world market in agricultural products was gaining in strength. The state-corporate international agro-feed regime simply understood agricultural products to be just like any other commodity, no more strategic and of no greater national importance than other goods which were traded openly on the world market. Thus to pry open markets – all markets, everywhere – was the overriding purpose of the WTO as shaped by the agro-feed regime.

The failure by the US and EU to abide by the obligations they appeared to accept with the agricultural agreement indicates that agro-regimes, by being cumulative, may carry seeds of conflicting logics, food drivers clashing with feed drivers. The feed lobby got the agricultural agreement in, the food lobby made sure that it was not implemented. With the advent of the agrofuel regime, such conflicts are likely to multiply, adding to the contradictions which already take place on the ground in the shape of land grabbing and power struggles over land resources.

## The climate regime and forests

The climate change discourse adds a new aspect to the fungibility of land areas and land-based resources, and this has a major impact on the agrofuel regime, leading to an intensification of the trend towards commoditization of agriculture and land-based resources. It also legitimizes "green grabbing", the acquisition of land purportedly to cater to ecological considerations (Corson and MacDonald 2012:273).

By recognizing that deforestation is one of the main drivers of climate change – 12 to 17 per cent of the global GHG emissions are related to logging, deforestation and unsustainable forestry (WRI 2005 for the lower figure covering only the South, and IPCC 2007 for the higher estimate) – forests were included in the climate negotiations through a mechanism which initially was called Reduced Emissions from Deforestation and Forest Degradation, REDD; subsequently, forest management and reforestation were added, yielding the acronym REDD+ (for REDD+ programs, see www.un-redd.org/). The idea is that forests should be left standing or at least managed in a way which sequesters carbon, and that countries who commit themselves to this will receive payment to make up for their foregone income. The carbon saved will be turned into "credits" to be sold on a market to corporations or governments which need to show that they have "reduced" their emissions, turning forest carbon, in the words of Conservation International, into an "asset class" and a "business segment" (Conservation International 2011:iv).

However, in order to be able to impact climate change, the payment for the non-use of forests must lead to a permanent improvement in the carbon cycle. But which government is able to credibly undertake such long-term commitments? Not without making protecting forests part of the constitution; and even so, the balance of powers may change to the benefit of the forces who want to turn forests into commodities just as any other land-based resource. The point to be made in this connection – the appropriation of ecological space and the ensuing land struggles – is that forest as climate control is yet a new competitor for the available land areas, not yet as important but with a potential for becoming more so as a new climate regime is negotiated.

A second issue in relation to REDD+, and also one which clearly ties in with my discussion of the fungibility of land areas, has to do with "leakage". As REDD+ projects block deforestation in one location, the price of land will be pushed up, and the paid property owners will be encouraged to open up new land elsewhere. An assessment of the few carbon sequestration projects to date shows leakage levels going up to 100 per cent or more: the money earned is spent on acquiring new lands, causing indirect land-use change of similar or even larger magnitudes (Wunder 2008:68). It is a parallel process to the one described in Chapter 3 regarding the chain effects from expanding sugarcane in Brazil's Cerrado.

## EU's raw materials diplomacy

Without referring to agro-regimes or to climate politics, Michael Klare noted ten years ago "the emergence of a new geography of conflict – a global landscape in which competition over vital resources is becoming the governing principle behind the disposition of and use of military power" (Klare 2002:214). His perspective was limited to the United States, but the European Union is also concerned about its future access to raw materials. In a statement by the European Commission in 2006, raw materials were singled out in menacing words:

> More than ever, Europe needs to import to export. Tackling restrictions on access to reources such as energy, metals and scrap, primary raw materials including certain agricultural materials, hides and skins must be a high priority. Measures taken by some of our biggest trading partners to restrict access to their supplies of these inputs are causing some EU industries major problems. Unless justified for security or environmental reasons, *restrictions on access to resources should be removed.*
>
> (European Commission 2006:7, italics added)

In the EU policy statement which followed in early 2011, the aggressive wording had been softened, but this cannot hide the fact that continuous and unhindered access to minerals and agricultural resources is a key concern to the EU. According to the Commission, the EU needs a "raw materials diplomacy" in order to secure a constant flow of primary commodities (European Commission 2011:11). This sounds neo-colonial, does it not, as if access to the resources which other countries harbour were a right of the EU.

The reason to worry, the European Commission explains, is that a high share of the worldwide production of "critical raw materials ... comes from a handful of countries", and it lists China, Russia, DR Congo and Brazil as the main suppliers. The "critical" resources contemplated by the Commission were antimony, beryllium, cobalt, fluorspar, gallium, germanium, graphite, indium, magnesium, niobium, platinum, rare earths, tantalum and tungsten (European Commission 2011:21); it has obviously not yet dawned on the Commission that land-based resources for the provisioning of food, feed, fibres, fuels and climate stability should be included.

Not only has the European Commission failed to grasp the real significance of the agrofuel regime; their list of problematic suppliers is also misleading, as we can gather from Table 6.7. Raw materials, be they minerals or agricultural, are controlled by countries and corporations in the North and, to a lesser extent, the South; they are not the sole purview of poor or unstable nations.

The EU's partial blindness is perhaps intentional: if essential raw materials and commodities are controlled by dictators and corrupt regimes, the EU could be forgiven for intervening. Just a step further, and we will encounter the argument that the EU is in its right to use violence to secure its needs; after all, war is the continuation of politics by other means, as Clausewitz famously mused in his influential study *On War* (originally published in German in 1832).

The same concern which defines the EU raw materials diplomacy – the wish to secure a continuous flow of primary commodities – may also be framed in pacific, non-confrontational terms, posing future conflicts as "risks" and "challenges". This is the approach of the global business community and its recently formed Risk Response Network (WEF 2011). The network, which is part of the World Economic Forum, WEF, underlines as one of three global "risk nexuses" climate change, food and water insecurity, and the volatility of energy prices. If this sounds familiar, it should: the WEF describes quite accurately the situation during the period leading up to the financial crisis of 2008 as well as its immediate aftermath. And indeed, the uninterrupted flow of food and other land-based resources to the North is threatened, but not primarily by a small number of unstable states rich in raw materials. Rather, the "risk nexus" here is that the global food-feed-fibre-fuel market is becoming more and more integrated, and hence more and more vulnerable, which in turn explains the intent of WEF, in tandem with the EU, to secure a continuous flow of raw materials.

## The underpinnings of the agrofuel regime

The agrofuel regime is global, but it would not have arisen had it not been fomented, regulated and financed by states, in coalition with national and international corporations, involving a mixture of perhaps unexpected participants, from civil society organizations to research institutions and universities (as discussed in Chapters 2 and 3).

It is common to view globalization as a phase of capitalist development where international financial institutions and corporations have taken over from weak and overrun governments. But, using sociologist Saskia Sassen's term (2006), we should recognize that the present stage – and the present agrofuel regime – is "multi-scalar", not national *or* global, private *or* public, but all of these at the same time. This may not sound like much of an insight, but what Sassen rescues out of the hype surrounding globalization is that the process is propelled to a considerable degree by national power (and not only by transnational institutions and corporations).

Intermediary actors play a crucial role in the establishment of this new agrofuel regime, symbolized by the promotion of agrofuels. Such "go-betweens" enable the appropriation of land areas and land-based resources, of which "green grab" is the latest addition: the use of ecological arguments to justify the appropriation of land areas and land-based resources. The go-betweens include consultancy firms and specialists in geographic information systems, supplying the map and the scientific garb needed to prepare for the grab, as well as experts in elaborating carbon offset interventions acceptable as REDD+ projects, and agents who negotiate land deals with local communities and governments (Fairhead *et al.* 2012).

To fathom all of these drivers and actors concurrently targeting land and land-based resources is not easy, as we are confronted by a complex and multi-scalar landscape – Sassen prefers the term "assemblage" – similar to what we saw in Chapters 2 and 3in connection with the introduction, legitimation and expansion of the sugarcane ethanol complex on national and global scales. The main point is that land as an essential and limited resource has attracted the attention of ever more actors, linking the national to the international, the private to the public, the North to the South, and mixing them all.

Such complexes, as we have seen, abound in the global agrofuel and land grabbing regimes, erasing the border that distinguishes domestic from international. A telling case is the push by the then Florida governor Jeb Bush to turn Miami into the "ethanol capital of the world", offering it as the gateway to the US market for Brazilian agro-businesses, led by UNICA, the Brazilian sugarcane industry association. In 2006, Jeb Bush went to Washington DC to convince his brother, President George W. Bush, that the US needed to adopt "a hemispheric wide approach to ethanol" with the catchy slogan "15 by 15": 15 billion gallons (57 billion litres) by the year 2015 (Hollander 2010:707). This appeared a bold goal then, but it was dwarfed by what later became the US mandate, 36 billion gallons (137 billion litres) by 2022.

To achieve his aim, Governor Bush had to show the US administration that Brazilian sugarcane ethanol was "environmental friendly" and that it qualified for supplying the US market, similar to UNICA's effort to convince the EU Commission (see Chapter 3).

This is yet another example of how the agrofuel regime relies on the climate change discourse in order to bring home the need to find a substitute for fossil fuels. It is through the ecological argument in favour of replacing fossil fuels by agrofuels that the new agro-regime comes of age, adorned with ecological credentials.

Questioning the scientific and ecological legitimacy of the agrofuel regime will encounter staunch resistance, as there are many stakeholders who have joined forces and tied their hopes – and their careers – to the alleged merits of agrofuels. Such alliances in the service of the agrofuel complex help explain the furious opposition I encountered in Brazil when I attempted to discuss the advisability of expanding sugarcane in the Cerrado. I pointed to the lack of firm knowledge about the impact on direct and indirect land-use change from expanding sugarcane, and suggested that this in turn questions the status of Brazilian ethanol as "climate neutral". On two separate occasions, Brazilian colleagues, fellow university scholars, got very upset and scolded me for raising the issue of land-use change. This was no business of mine, I was told in unequivocal words:

"We will do with the Amazon as we like! You people from Europe have nothing to teach us after you have cut down all your own forests! A Amazônia é nossa! The Amazon belongs to us!" What ignited such outbursts, I believe, is that my academic colleagues correctly detected criticism of the new agrofuel regime and felt themselves, as part of the agrofuel complex, implicated.

If the term "complex" brings the farewell speech of the US President Eisenhower to mind, this is intentional (Eisenhower 1961). Eisenhower talked of two complexes in his last message to the American people before leaving the presidency to his successor John F Kennedy, in January 1961, but it is only one side of his admonition which has remained in the public mind. Eisenhower stressed that the "conjunction of an immense military establishment and a large arms industry is new in the American experience"; this military-industrial complex was exerting "total influence – economic, political, even spiritual ... in every city, every State house, every office of the Federal government", and Eisenhower warned that this complex could attain "unwarranted influence" resulting in a "potential for the disastrous rise of misplaced power".

What is not equally well remembered, however, is that Eisenhower saw a twin danger in the rise of the "scientific-technological elite" to whom "a government contract becomes virtually a substitute for intellectual curiosity" in Eisenhower's well-chosen words. What the agrofuel regime proves is that these two complexes have joined forces: the new agrofuel regime needs the benediction of the scientific-technological elite.

## Land-use change in the future: what we can expect

It is not only my two assumptions – peak oil, peak soil – which tell us that the conflicts over land use will increase; three already manifest tendencies indicate that land struggles will intensify. First, agricultural productivity increase appears to have reached its limits. The annual increase in area productivity of cereal production – wheat, maize and rice, the mainstay of the global diet – has declined decade by decade during the last 40 years: 3.7 per cent in the 1960s, 2.5 in the 1970s, 1.4 in the 1980s, and 1.1 per cent in the period 1990–2001 (FAO 2006:5). For the coming 40 years, i.e. until 2050, this trend is expected to continue, and only 0.9 per cent annual production growth from 2030 to 2050 is expected (Bruinsma 2009:6). This does not mean that production is decreasing, only that we cannot count on growth rates to keep up with the ever-increasing demand for food and feed, let alone hope that arable land will be freed up to allow an equally urgent expansion of the production of fibres, fuels and forests.

Second, the possibility of replacing fossil fuels with land-based renewables will encounter limitations, as the renewable alternatives are much less area-efficient than the fossil alternatives they replace. Put differently: the "power density" of renewables is low. While fossil fuels have a power density of 100 or 1,000 watts per square metre, biomass energy on average is well below $1 W/m^2$, and US maize ethanol only achieves $0.22 W/m^2$ (Smil 2005:22). Thus, a shift from fossil to agrofuels has the exact opposite implication in area terms compared to the previous shift from agrofuels to fossil fuels: then, lower-density was replaced by higher-density; now, we are proposing to replace higher by lower. Conclusion: the strain on available land areas will grow stronger still.

Third, it is not only agriculture which will be seeking to expand its area; urbanization will also take a toll, especially on lands located close to today's population centres. With a growing world population and continuing urbanization, urban areas are expected to triple in the coming 20 years (compared to the year 2000), turning another 121 million hectares into concrete by 2030 (Seto *et al.* 2012). This is a large chunk out of what today to a large extent are agriculturally productive areas of high value in close proximity to markets, often with access to infrastructure (most importantly transport and irrigation). In other words, the wave of urbanization will not only take over agricultural lands, it is also likely to speed up the process of indirect land-use change as high-revenue land close to urban centres is transformed into land acquisitions in lower-priced regions further afield.

If increases in productivity – be they in food, feed, fibres or fuels – must be ruled out as a solution to the steeply rising demand for land areas and land-based resources, the result – in the absence of dramatic dietary change or significant technical breakthroughs – will most likely be that ever more land areas are deforested to make room for the renewable resources which are demanded by the new agrofuel regime. Table 8.4 shows the impressive areas cleared historically, in all continents, to create the global landscape we have today of 1,500 hectares of crop land.

The most important data to note in Table 8.4 are that Europe and North America during the last period, 1950–1980, had decreasing areas dedicated to crop lands as reforestation occurred, while the rest of the world went in the opposite direction and saw an increase in the areas cleared for crops.

With this metric we can also see a displacement of land use: the increase in crop lands in the South enables a decrease in the Centre. The measures of ecologically unequal exchange of land indicate how the contradiction is resolved: by the North appropriating the ecological space it requires.

This shift of crop lands from the North to the South has continued unabated, as shown by satellite images of land-use change from 1995 to 2007, that is the period

*Table 8.4* Crop land changes, 1700–1980, million hectares

|                        | 1700–1800 | 1800–1920 | 1920–1950 | 1950–1980 |
|------------------------|-----------|-----------|-----------|-----------|
| Africa and Middle East | 11        | 56        | 71        | 127       |
| Asia                   | 38        | 90        | 65        | 120       |
| Europe                 | 30        | 50        | 5         | −15       |
| Latin America          | 4         | 34        | 42        | 55        |
| North America          | 6         | 170       | 27        | −3        |
| Russia, Oceania        | 27        | 132       | 47        | 47        |
| **Total**              | **116**   | **532**   | **257**   | **588**   |

Source: Based on Grübler 1998, Table 5.3.

following the last one shown in Table 8.4: in the North, agricultural areas decreased, while they increased in the South. During these years, crops and pastures of the North declined by as much as 412 million hectares, while they simultaneously increased in the South by an estimated 400 million hectares (Gibbs *et al.* 2010:16736). Again, the appropriation of ecological space is targeting the South.

In a business-as-usual scenario, this tendency can be expected to hold. The expansion of agricultural lands during the last decades of the twentieth century – that is, during the period following the long-term land-use change described in Table 8.4 – has continued, and it takes place mostly at the expense of existing forests, not on pastures. Fifty-five per cent of the total expansion of agricultural lands from 1980 to 2000 occurred at the expense of intact forests, and a further 28 per cent replaced "disturbed forests", with all in all approximately 80 million hectares of forests turned into crop lands (Gibbs *et al.* 2010, Figure 2). In general, then – and contrary to what we saw in connection with the expansion of sugarcane cultivation in Brazil in Chapter 3 – crop lands do not expand over previously cleared lands such as pastures, but are one of the main drivers of deforestation, and this process takes place more or less equally on all the continents and regions of the South. It is the general trend.

Such displacement is now made part of the scenarios for feeding the world's socio-ecological metabolic process. The UN Food and Agriculture Organization is counting on increasing land use in the South and decreasing in the North, following the pattern we have seen during the last 60 years: while Africa and Latin America will deforest an estimated 120 million hectares by 2050, Europe and North America are estimated to re-forest 50 million hectares. The net outcome is predicted to be an expansion of arable lands of 70 million hectares (FAO 2009c:9). The World Bank, while also recognizing the trend to reforestation in the North, presents an even larger land-use change which it alarmingly dubs "conservative" of 120–240 million hectares of new crop lands by 2030, mostly in Latin America and Africa (World Bank 2011:6).

This is the most likely tendency, then: although deforestation may be slowing down compared to the post-World War II period, it will still go on at a frightening pace. And it may get much worse, if not even the reduced productivity increases which are factored into these scenarios materialize. A counterfactual calculation shows the dimension of the problem. In the absence of productivity gains from 1961 to 2005, the agricultural land areas needed to feed today's population would have been 1.8 billion hectares larger than they in fact are. In other words, today's metabolic regime, with yesterday's area productivity, would have required over twice today's crop lands (which are 1.5 billion hectares). In the future, given present trends, and discounting an improvement in productivity of the magnitude we had during the second half of the twentieth century, another 1.5–2 billion hectares will be needed by 2050, once again more than doubling the global crop lands of today (*Nature* 2010:853).

Thus, to the extent that there have been land areas spared from exploitation, we should be grateful for the impressive improvement in productivity during the last 50 years. But, to repeat, this is not something we can take for granted henceforth.

## Financialization of land

Recently the World Bank, together with the International Fund for Agricultural Development, the UN Conference on Trade and Development, and the UN Food and Agriculture Organization, launched a set of investment rules under the ambitious heading "Principles for Responsible Agricultural Investments which Respect Rights, Livelihoods and Resources" (RAI 2012). However, according to the UN special rapporteur on the right to food, Olivier de Schutter, these principles are a "checklist of how to destroy the global peasantry responsibly" (de Schutter 2011:275), and a civil society organization (CSO) and peasant coalition holds that the principles, far from being responsible, only amount to greenwashing: "a move to try to legitimize what is absolutely unacceptable: the long-term-corporate (foreign and domestic) takeover of rural people's farmlands" (Via Campesina *et al.* 2010:1–2).

In this way, CSOs and peasant organizations are distancing themselves from the financialization and commodification of land, a stand which brings to mind the vehemence with which the philosopher and historian Karl Polanyi in 1944 argued against the general tendency to commodify "essential elements" such as labour, land, and money, three "fictitious commodities" which were not to be left at the mercy of the market without proper regulation and institutions. Polanyi wrote in 1944, influenced by the catastrophes of World War II:

> What we call land is an element of nature inextricably interwoven with man's institutions. To isolate it and form a market out of it was perhaps the weirdest of all undertakings of our ancestors.... Undoubtedly, labor, land, and money markets are essential to a market economy. But no society could stand the effects of such a system of crude fictions [i.e. that labor, land and money are commodities] even for the shortest stretch of time unless its human and natural substance as well as its business organization was protected against the ravages of this satanic mill.
>
> (Polanyi 2002/1944:187, 76–77)

Keynes, influenced by the crash of Wall Street in 1929 and the financial breakdown of the 1930s, expressed similar apprehension should money be considered to be just like any commodity. In a celebrated section of his General Theory, he says:

> Speculators may do no harm as bubbles on a steady stream of enterprise. But the position is serious when enterprise becomes the bubble on a whirlpool of speculation. When the capital development of a country becomes a by-product of the activities of a casino, the job is likely to be ill-done.
>
> (Keynes 2007/1936:142–143)

State control of land is no hedge against land appropriation, as we have seen; on the contrary, it is thanks to public rule over land resources that large land deals can so easily and swiftly be brokered with foreign and domestic investors. It does not matter that customary rights may be guaranteed, not even if they are written into the constitution; governments in the South regularly dispose of lands over which they have no formal dominion (see Wily 2011 on land grabbing in Africa).

But governments often assume that they are representing a higher justice than the law, or they simply interpret the law in favour of "change" and "progress", as they define it. We saw in Chapter 7 how the Indian Supreme Court counterposed the interests of the few and marginalized against the benefits of development to the overwhelming majority of the Indian population in order to approve illicit shipbreaking on Indian shores. In less conciliatory language, Alan García, then president of Peru, warned Peru's indigenous population not to stand in the way of large-scale investments in land and mining, telling them in 2007 in the Peruvian daily *El Comércio* to learn from the "experience of the successful peoples, the Germans, the Japanese, the Koreans, and many more":

> Reality teaches us that we should put the resources which we do not use to work and expend more effort … indigenous people do not wear a crown, they are not first class citizens who can tell us – 400,000 natives to 28 million Peruvians – that you have no right to come here, no way. It is a serious mistake and anyone who thinks like this wants to push us back to irrationality and to our primitive past.
>
> (quoted in Benavides 2010:7–8)

The tradition of disregarding the land use by people held to be "backwards" or "inferior" goes a long way back, of course, and has not always need to rely on Geographic Information Systems; Friedrich Engels in 1844 ridiculed the Malthusian idea of population pressure on limited land as "absurd", as there was enough "waste land" available in the Mississippi valley to allow the "transplantation" of the whole population of Europe, and he went on to stress that "no more than one-third of the Earth can be considered cultivated" and that "the production of this third itself can be raised six fold and more by the application of improvements already known" (Engels 1844:19–20). I detect here a similar outlook to the one which 128 years later made Arghiri Emmanuel lament that the Earth was seriously under-utilized (see Chapter 4).

## Return to the land

We are entering a new age where land is coming to the fore once again, an era which I believe will bear a resemblance to the conflicts which accompanied the undoing of the laws valid for all times which Malthus thought he established in 1798. As the limits to growth then were overcome by a combination of appropriation of land areas (colonialism) and the substitution of land-based energy for fossil fuels (coal and later oil), the limits today may temporarily be stretched through environmental load displacement and the various shapes of appropriation of ecological space which I have documented in this book.

This, then, heralds the return to the land as a key scarce resource needed for capital accumulation, economic growth and development. Although Malthus was wrong for 200 years, he is now right, at least if my two underlying assumptions – no fossil fuels, no deforestation – are respected.

Such thoughts were behind my initial argument in favour of re-introducing a Malthusian perspective, and for not rejecting the label "neo-Malthusian", at the outset of this study. Here, I am once again in the company of Georg Borgström. Although he in the 1950s tried to dissociate himself from Malthus – he then considered "Malthusian" an insult and was afraid that he would be dismissed in the public debate should he be associated with the "old priest" (Linnér 1998:114 and 206) – a decade later Borgström had changed his opinion and now celebrated Malthus as a "mathematician and economist, not at all 'a poor priest led astray', who in simple and clear words and with mathematical precision had formulated the unquestionable limit to the size of humanity established by the availability of food" (Borgström 1964:258). Apparently, Borgström had become more self-assured in the intervening years, and now supported his own ideas by admiringly referring to Malthus's "clear-sightedness" in establishing a "final limit to the extension of mankind" (Borgström 1964:260).

I am not sure whether Borgström refers to the "young" Malthus – who at 32 years of age published his *Essay on the Principle of Population* anonymously in 1798 – or to the "mature" Malthus, who five years later in a revised edition of his Essay made a clear statement against expropriating lands and ousting indigenous people overseas to make room for the surplus population of Europe. Possibly writing in reply to Benjamin Franklin, who in 1755 had contemplated replacing "all Blacks and Tawneys" by whites, Malthus said:

> There are many parts of the globe, indeed, hitherto uncultivated, and almost unoccupied; but the right to exterminating, or driving into a corner where they must starve, even the inhabitants of these thinly-peopled regions, will be questioned in a moral view.... To exterminate the inhabitants of the greatest part of Asia and Africa, is a thought that could not be admitted for a moment.
>
> (quoted in Bashford 2012:105)

Historian Alison Bashford comments that if Malthus had renamed his later versions instead of keeping the original title, more readers would be familiar with how his thinking on this subject evolved. As it is, most readers, including myself, and most contemporary publishers feel satisfied with the first, short edition, and we are thus liable not only to miss that Malthus did oppose the colonial "solution" to the contradiction of population–agriculture, but also that his words – driving people into a corner – sound eerily relevant today in relation to the appropriation of ecological space in general, and land grabbing in particular.

In my view, then, the appropriation of ecological space should be seen, to paraphrase Clausewitz, as a continuation by other means of the colonial route of escape from the restrictions imposed by limited land areas and competition for land-based resources.

# References

All electronic links accessed January 2013.

Adriaanse, A., Bringezu, S., Hammond, A., Moriguchi, Y., Roderburg, E., Rogich, D. and Schütz, H. (1997): *Resources Flows: The Material Basis of Industrial Economies*, WRI/Wuppertal Institute/Netherlands Ministry of Housing, Spatial Planning and Environment, National Institute for Environmental Studies.

Aguiar, D.A., Adami, M., Rudorff, B.F.T., Sugawara, L.M. and Freitas, R.M. (2009): *Availiação da conversão do uso e ocupação do solo para cana-de-açúcar utilizando imagens de sensoriamento remoto* [Assessment of land-use change for sugarcane by remote sensing], Anais XIV Simpósio de Sensoriamento Remoto, Natal.

Alston, L.J. and Mueller, B. (2007): "Legal Reserve Requirements in Brazilian Forests: Path Dependent Evolution of de facto Legislation", *Revista Economia Selecta* 8(4):25–53.

Alves, F. (2006): "Por que morrem os cortadores de cana?" [Why are the cane cutters dying?], *Saúde e Sociedade* 15(3):90–98.

Amann, C., Bruckner, W., Fischer-Kowalski, M. and Grünbühel, C. (2002): *Material Flow Accounting in Amazônia*, Social Ecology Working Paper 63, Vienna: Institute of Social Ecology, IFF.

Amin, S. (1976): *Unequal Development: An Essay on the Social Formations of Peripheral Capitalism*. New York: Monthly Review Press.

Andrew, R., Peters, G.P. and Lennox, J. (2009): "Approximation and Regional Aggregation in MRIO Analysis for National Carbon Footprint Accounting", *Economic Systems Research* 21(3):311–335.

Anseeuw, W., Alden Wilý, L., Cotula, L. and Taylor, M. (2012): *Land Rights and the Rush for Land*, IIEED/Cirad/International Land Coalition, www.landcoalition.org/sites/default/files/publication/1205/ILC%20GSR%20report_ENG.pdf.

Arezki, R., Deininger, K. and Selod, H. (2011): *What Drives the Global Land Rush?* IMF Working Paper WP/11/251, Washington, DC.

Assad de Ávila, S.R.S., de Ávila, M.L. and Altafin, I. (2010): *Efeitos sócio-económicos da expansão da cana-de-açúcar no Vale do São Patrício* [Socio-economic impact of the expansion of sugarcane in the São Patrício valley], Universidade de Brasília.

Augustin, C.E. (2012): "Can Brazilian Agriculture Create Prosperity in Africa?", *Sustainable Business Forum*, 18 October, http://sustainablebusinessforum.com/marcgunther/54540/can-brazilian-agribusiness-create-prosperity-africa.

Baffes, J. and Haniotis, T. (2010): *Placing the 2006/08 Commodity Price Boom into Perspective*, Policy Research Working Paper 5371, Washington, DC: World Bank.

BAN [Basel Action Network] (2011): *Scrapping Lives: The Export of Toxic Ships to Asia*, http://ban.org/library/factsheet.html.

Baran, P. (1967): *The Political Economy of Growth*. New York: Monthly Review Press.

Bashford, A. (2012): "Malthus and Colonial History", *Journal of Australian Studies* 36(1):99–110.

Benavides, M. (2010): "Amazonía peruana: El choque de dos visiones de desarrollo – La protesta indígena del 2008 y 2009 frente a los decretos legislativos que afectaban sus territorio" [The Peruvian Amazon: Conflicting visions of development – Indigenous protests in 2008 and 2009 against legal decrees concerning their territory], Annual World Bank Land Policy and Administration Conference, http://siteresources.worldbank.org/EXTARD/Resources/336681–1236436879081/BenavidesPaper.pdf.

Berglund, M. (2011): *Green Growth? A Consumption Perspective on Swedish Environmental Impact Trends Using Input-Output Analysis*, Uppsala University, http://uu.diva-portal.org/smash/get/diva2:436275/FULLTEXT01.

Berndes, G., Bird, N. and Cowie, A. (2010): *Bioenergy, Land Use Change and Climate Change Mitigation*, IEA Bioenergy ExCo 2010(03).

Berndes, G., Hoogwijk, M. and van den Boek, R. (2003): "The Contribution of Biomass in the Future Global Energy Supply: A Review of 17 Studies", *Biomass and Bioenergy* 25:1–28.

Bioenergia (2009): "O etanol pode ser uma 'commodity'" [Ethanol could become a commodity], *Revista brasileira de bioenergia* 8:36–37.

BNDES (2010): *O BNDES e a agroindústria*, Informe Setorial No. 18, www.bndes.gov.br/SiteBNDES/export/sites/default/bndes_pt/Galerias/Arquivos/conhecimento/setorial/informe-18AI.pdf.

BNDES and CGEE [Centro de Gestão e Estudos Estratégicos] (2008): *Bioetanol de cana-de-açucar: Energia para o desenvolvimento sustentável* [Sugarcane bioethanol: Energy for sustainable development], www.bioetanoldecana.org/pt/download/bioetanol.pdf.

Borgström, G. (1964): *Gränser för vår tillvaro* [The limits of our existence]. Borås: LTs Förlag.

Borgström Hansson, C. (2003): *Misplaced Concreteness and Concrete Places: Critical Analyses of Divergent Discourses on Sustainability*, Lund Studies in Human Ecology 7, Lund University.

Borras, S.M., McMichael, P. and Scoones, I. (2010): "The Politics of Biofuels – Land and Agrarian Change: Editors' Introduction", *Journal of Peasant Studies* 37(4):575–592.

Borras Jr., S.M., Franco, J.C., Gómez, S., Kay, C. and Spoor, M. (2012): "Land Grabbing in Latin America and the Caribbean", *Journal of Peasant Studies* 39(3–4):845–872.

Borras Jr., S.M., Hall, R., Scoones, I., White, B. and Wolford, W. (2011): "Towards a Better Understanding of Global Land Grabbing: An Editorial Introduction", *Journal of Peasant Studies* 38(2):209–216.

Boserup, E. (1965): *The Conditions of Agricultural Growth: The Economics of Agrarian Change under Population Pressure*. London: George Allen and Unwin.

Boyden, S., Millar, S., Newcombe, K. and O'Neill, B. (1981): *The Ecology of a City and Its People: The Case of Hong Kong*. Canberra: Australian National University Press.

Brahmbhatt, M. and Canuto, O. (2010): *Natural Resources and Development Strategies After the Crisis*, Economic Premise No 1, Washington, DC: World Bank.

Brazilian Academy of Sciences (2010): "ABC e SBPC manifestam preocupação com mudanças propostas ao Código Florestal" [ABC and SBPC preoccupied by proposed modifications of the forest code], www.abc.org.br/article.php3?id_article=719.

Brown, L. and Kane, H. (1995): *Full House: Reassessing the Earth's Population Carrying Capacity*. London: Earthscan.

Bruinsma, J. (2009): *The Resource Outlook to 2050: By How Much Do Land and Crop Yields Need to Increase by 2050?* Expert Meeting on How to Feed the World in 2050, FAO, Rome, ftp://ftp.fao.org/docrep/fao/012/ak971e/ak971e00.pdf.

Brunnermeier, S. and Levinson, A. (2004): "Examining the Evidence on Environmental Regulations and Industry Location", *The Journal of Environment and Development* 13(1):6–41.

Bunker, S.G. (1985): *Underdeveloping the Amazon: Extraction, Unequal Exchange, and the Failure of the Modern State.* Chicago: University of Chicago Press.

Bunker, S.G. and Ciccantell, P.S. (2005): *Globalization and the Race for Resources.* Baltimore: Johns Hopkins University Press.

Bustamente, M.M.C., Nobre, C.A., Smeraldi, R., de Siqueira Pinto, A., Dutra de Aguiar, A.P., Ometto, J.P.H.B., Longo, K., Guimarães Ferreira, L., Barioni, L.G. and May, P. (undated): *Resumo e principais conclusões: Estimativa de emissões recentes de gases de efeito estufa pela pecuária no Brasil* [Summary and main conclusions: Estimates of recent greenhouse gas emissions by livestock in Brazil], www.inpe.br/noticias/arquivos/pdf/Resumo_Principais_Conclusoes_emissoes_da_pecuaria_vfinalJean.pdf.

Buyny, S. and Lauber, U. (2010): *Environmental-Economic Accounting: Further Development of the Indicator "Raw Material Productivity" in the National Strategy for Sustainable Development,* Federal Statistical Office of Germany, Wiesbaden, www.destatis.de/EN/Publications/Specialized/EnvironmentalEconomicAccounting/RawMaterialsProductivity.pdf?__blob=publicationFile.

Câmara dos Deputados (1999): *Projeto de Lei No 1.876,* http://imagem.camara.gov.br/MostraIntegraImagem.asp?strSiglaProp=PLandintProp=1876andintAnoProp=1999andintParteProp=1.

Carlsson-Kanyama, A., Assefa, G., Peters, G. and Wadeskog, A. (2007): *Koldioxidutsläpp till följd av Sveriges import och konsumtion* [Carbon Emissions Related to Swedish Imports and Consumption]. Stockholm: Royal Institute of Technology, www.ima.kth.se/eng/respublic/CO2_utslaepp_import_konsumtion.pdf.

Catton, W.R. (1980): *Overshoot: The Ecological Basis of Revolutionary Change.* Urbana, IL: University of Illinois Press.

CE Delft (2008): *Agricultural Land Availability and Demand in 2020,* AEA Technology Managed Study for the *Gallagher Review,* Delft, www.cedelft.eu/art/uploads/file/08_4723_29.pdf.

Chapagain, A.K. and Hoekstra, A.Y. (2004): *Water Footprints of Nations,* Volume 1: *Main Report,* Value of Water Research Series No. 16, UNESCO-IHE.

Clark, B. and Foster, J.B. (2012): "Guano: The Global Metabolic Rift and the Fertilizer Trade", in Hornborg, A., Clark, B. and Hermele, K., eds: *Ecology and Power: Struggles over Land and Material Resources in the Past, Present and Future.* Abingdon: Routledge.

Cleveland, C.J. and O'Connor, P.A. (2011): "Energy Return on Investment (EROI) of Oil Shale", *Sustainability* 3:283–298, www.mdpi.com/journal/sustainability/special_issues/New_Studies_EROI.

Cohen, J.E. (1995): *How Many People Can the Earth Support?* New York: Norton.

Cohen, M.J. and Garrett, J.L. (2009): *The Food Price Crisis and Urban Food (In)Security,* IIED http://pubs.iied.org/pdfs/10574IIED.pdf.

Cole, M.A., Elliott, R.J.R. and Strobl, E. (2008): "The Environmental Performance of Firms: The Role of Foreign Ownership, Training and Experience", *Ecological Economics* 65:538–546.

Compromisso nacional para aperfeiçoar as condições de trabalho na cana-de-açúcar [National agreement to improve working conditions in the sugarcane fields] (2009), http://www.secretariageral.gov.br/.arquivos/publicacaocanadeacucar.pdf.

Conab (2010): *Acompanhamento da Safra Brasileira* [Brazilian sugarcane harvest monitor], Companhia Nacional de Abastecimento, Safra 2010/2011, Segundo Levantamento, Brasília.

Conservation International (2011): *Project Developer's Guidebook to VCS REDD Methodologies*, www.conservation.org/about/centers_programs/carbon_fund/Documents/project_developers_guide_to_vcs_redd_11282011FINAL.pdf.

Convenção coletiva de trabalho do setor canavierio goiano 2010 [Collective agreement for the sugarcane sector in Goiás 2010], FETAEG, Goiânia.

Copeland, B.R. and Taylor, M.S. (2004): "Trade, Growth and the Environment", *Journal of Economic Literature* 42(1):7–71.

Corson, C. and MacDonald, K.I. (2012): "Enclosing the Global Commons: The Convention on Biological Diversity and Green Grabbing", *Journal of Peasant Studies* 39(2):263–283.

Cotula, L. (2012): "The International Political Economy of the Global Land Rush: A Critical Appraisal of Trends, Scale, Geography and Drivers", *Journal of Peasant Studies* 39(3–4):649–680.

CPT [Comissão Pastoral da Terra] (2010): *Conflitos no campo Brasil 2009* [Rural struggles in Brazil 2009], www.cptnacional.org.br/index.php?option=com_jdownloadsandItemid=23andtask=finishandcid=131andcatid=4.

Cronon, W. (1991): *Nature's Metropolis: Chicago and the Great West*. New York: Norton.

Cruz, R. (2010): "Abrindo a porteira do desmatamento" [Opening the door to deforestation], *Le Monde Diplomatique Brasil*, June.

Daily, G., Dasgupta, P., Bolin, B., Crosson, P., du Guerny, J., Ehrlich, P., Folke, C., Jansson, A.M., Jansson, B.-O., Kautsky, N., Kinzig, A., Levin, S., Mäler, K.-G., Pinstrup-Andersen, P., Siniscalco, D. and Walker, B. (1998): "Food Production, Population Growth, and the Environment", *Science* (281)5381:1291–1292.

Dale, V.H., Kline, K.L., Wiens, J. and Fargione, J. (2010): *Biofuels: Implications for Land Use and Biodiversity*, Biofuels and Sustainability Reports, Ecological Society of America, www.esa.org/biofuelsreports/files/ESA%20Biofuels%20Report_VH%20Dale%20et%20al.pdf.

Daly, H.E. (1992/1977): *Steady-State Economics*. London: Earthscan.

Daly, H.E. (1998): "The Return of Lauderdale's Paradox", *Ecological Economics* 25:21–23.

Datt, M., Hoekman, B. and Malouche, M. (2011): *Taking Stock of Trade Protectionism since 2008*, Economic Premise 72, Washington, DC: World Bank.

Dauvergne, P. and Neville, K.J. (2010): "Forests, Food, and Fuel in the Tropics: The Uneven Social and Ecological Consequences of the Emerging Political Economy of Biofuels", *Journal of Peasant Studies* 37(4):631–660.

Davis, M. (2002): *Late Victorian Holocausts: El Niño Famines and the Making of the Third World*. London:Verso.

Demaria, F. (2010): "Shipbreaking at Alang-Sosiya (India): An Ecological Distribution Conflict", *Ecological Economics* 70:250–260.

de Schutter, O. (2011): "How Not to Think of Land-Grabbing: Three Critiques of Large-Scale Investments in Farmland", *Journal of Peasant Studies* 38(2):249–279.

Dittrich, M. and Bringezu, S. (2010): "The Physical Dimension of International Trade, Part 1: Direct Global Flows Between 1962 and 2005", *Ecological Economics* 69:1838–1847.

Dittrich, M., Giljum, S., Polzin, C., Lutter, S. and Bringezu, S. (2011): *Resource Use and Resource Efficiency in Emerging Economies: Trends Over the Past 20 Years*, Working Paper 12, Seri, Vienna.

Dyson, T. (1999): "World Food Trends and Prospects to 2025", *Proceedings of the National Academy of Sciences*, 96:5929–5936.

Eickhout, B., van den Born, G.J., Notenboom, J., van Oorschot, M., Ros, J.P.M., van Vuuren, D.P. and Westhoek, H.J. (2008): *Local and Global Consequences of the EU Renewable Directive for Biofuels*, Milieu en Natuur Planbureau, www.pbl.nl/sites/default/files/cms/publicaties/500143001.pdf.

Eisenhower, D.D. (1961): Farewell address, 17 January 1961, www.ourdocuments.gov/doc.php?flash=trueanddoc=90.

Eisenmenger, N. (2008): *A Biophysical View on Trade and the International Division of Labour*, PhD dissertation, Vienna: Institute of Social Ecology.

Embrapa (2008): *IV plano diretor da Embrapa Cerrados 2008–2011–2023* [IV general plan of Embrapa for the Cerrados 2008–2011–2023] Ministério da Agricultura, Pecuária e Abastecimento, Brasília.

Emmanuel, A. (1972): *Unequal Exchange: A Study of the Imperialism of Trade*. New York: Monthly Review Press.

Energy Watch Group (2007): *Coal: Resources and Future Production*, www.energy-watchgroup.org/fileadmin/global/pdf/EWG_Report_Coal_10–07–2007ms.pdf.

Engels, F. (1844): "Outlines of a Critique of Political Economy", *Deutsch-Französiche Jahrbücher*, www.marxists.org/archive/marx/works/1844/df-jahrbucher/outlines.htm.

EPA (2010): *EPA Finalizes Regulations for the National Renewable Fuel Standard Program for 2010 and Beyond*, www.epa.gov/oms/renewablefuels/420f10007.pdf.

Erb, K.H., Haberl, H., Krausmann, F., Lauk, C., Plutzar, C., Steinberger, J.K., Müller, C., Bondeau, A., Waha, K. and Pollack, G. (2009a): *Eating the Planet: Feeding and Fuelling the World Sustainably, Fairly and Humanely – A Scoping Study*, Social Ecology Working Paper 116, Vienna: Institute of Social Ecology.

Erb, K.H., Krausmann, F., Lucht, W. and Haberl, H. (2009b): "Embodied HANPP: Mapping the Spatial Disconnect between Global Biomass Production and Consumption", *Ecological Economics* 69:328–334.

ETBC [Electronics Take Back Coalition] (2012): *Facts and Figures on E-waste and Recycling*, www.electronicstakeback.com/hold-manufacturers-accountable/recycling-report-card/.

European Commission (2006): *Global Europe: Competing in the World*, http://trade.ec.europa.eu/doclib/docs/2006/october/tradoc_130376.pdf.

European Commission (2010): *Report from the Commission on Indirect Land-Use Change Related to Biofuels and Bioliquids*, COM (2010)811 final, http://eur-lex.europa.eu/LexUriServ/LexUriServ.do?uri=COM:2010:0811:FIN:EN:PDF.

European Commission (2011): *Tackling the Challenges in Commodity Markets and on Raw Materials*, COM (2011)25 final, 2 February, http://eur-lex.europa.eu/LexUriServ/LexUriServ.do?uri=COM:2011:0025:FIN:EN:PDF.

European Commission (2012): Proposal for a Directive of the European Parliament and of the Council amending Directive 98/70/EC relating to the Quality of Petrol and Diesel Fuels and amending Directive 2009/28/EC on the Promotion of the Use of Energy from Renewable Sources, http://ec.europa.eu/clima/policies/transport/fuel/docs/com_2012_595_en.pdf.

European Union (2009): Directive 2009/28/EC of the European Parliament and of the Council of 23 April 2009 on the Promotion of the Use of Energy from Renewable

Sources, http://eur-lex.europa.eu/LexUriServ/LexUriServ.do?uri=OJ:L:2009:140:0016 :0062:en:PDF.

Eurostat (2011): *Economy-wide Material Flows: European Countries Required More Materials Between 2000 and 2007*, Statistics in Focus 9/201, http://epp.eurostat.ec. europa.eu/cache/ITY_OFFPUB/KS-SF-11–009/EN/KS-SF-11–009-EN.PDF.

Fairhead, J., Leach, M. and Scoones, I. (2012): "Green Grabbing: A New Appropriation of Nature?" *Journal of Peasant Studies* 39(2):237–261.

FAO (2004): *The State of Agricultural Commodity Markets*, ftp://ftp.fao.org/docrep/ fao/007/y5419e/y5419e00.pdf.

FAO (2005): *Global Forest Resources Assessment 2005*, http://foris.fao.org/static/data/ fra2005/kf/common/GlobalForestA4-ENsmall.pdf.

FAO (2006): *World Agriculture: Towards 2030/2050 – Prospects for Food, Nutrition, Agriculture and Major Commodity Groups, Interim Report*, www.fao.org/fileadmin/ user_upload/esag/docs/Interim_report_AT2050web.pdf.

FAO (2008): *The State of Food and Agriculture: Biofuels – Prospects, Risks and Opportunities*, ftp://ftp.fao.org/docrep/fao/011/i0100e/i0100e.pdf.

FAO (2009a): *The Market and Food Security Implications of the Development of Biofuel Production*, ftp://ftp.fao.org/docrep/fao/meeting/016/k4477e.pdf.

FAO (2009b): *The State of Agricultural Commodity Markets: High Food Prices and the Food Crisis – Experiences and Lessons Learned*, ftp://ftp.fao.org/docrep/fao/012/ i0854e/i0854e.pdf.

FAO (2009c): *How to Feed the World in 2050*, High-Level Expert Forum, Rome, www. fao.org/fileadmin/templates/wsfs/docs/expert_paper/How_to_Feed_the_World_ in_2050.pdf.

FAO (2011): *The State of Food and Agriculture 2010–2011*, www.fao.org/docrep/013/ i2050e/i2050e.pdf.

FAO (2012a): *FAO Food Price Index*, www.fao.org/worldfoodsituation/wfs-home/food-pricesindex/en/.

FAO (2012b): *Statistical Yearbook 2012*, Rome.

FAO (2012c): *Cereal Production, Utilization and Stocks*, www.fao.org/worldfoodsituation/wfs-home/csdb/en/.

Fargione, J., Hill, J., Tilman, D., Polasky, S. and Hawthorne, P. (2008): "Land Clearing and the Biofuel Carbon Debt", *Science* 319:1235–1237.

FASE [Federação de Órgãos para Assistência Social e Educacional] (2008): "Amazônia: sob ação do fogo e da motoserra" [The Amazon under fire and chain saws], *Le Monde Diplomatique Brasil*, April.

Fearnside, P.M. (2008): "The Roles and Movements of Actors in the Deforestation of Brazilian Amazonia", *Ecology and Society* 13(1).

*Financial Times* (2009): "Madagascar Scraps Daewoo Farm Deal", 18 March, www. ft.com/cms/s/0/7e133310–13ba-11de-9e32–0000779fd2ac.html#axzz2EHbZEb8a.

Fischer, G., Teixeira, E., Tothne Hizsnyik, E. and van Velthuizen (2008): "Land Use Dynamics and Sugarcane Production", in Zuurbier, P. and van den Vooren, J., eds: *Sugarcane Ethanol: Contribution to Climate Change Mitigation and the Environment*, Wageningen: Wageningen Academic Publishers.

Fischer-Kowalski, M., Haberl, H. and Krausmann, F. (2007): "Conclusions: Likely and Unlikely Pasts, Possible and Impossible Futures", in Fischer-Kowalski, M. and Haberl, H., eds: *Socioecological Transitions and Global Change*. Cheltenham: Edward Elgar.

Foley, J.A., Ramankutty, N., Brauman, K.A., Cassidy, E.S., Gerber, J.S., Johnston, M., Mueller, N.D., O'Connel, C., Ray, D.K., West, P.C., Balzer, C., Bennet, E.M.,

Carpenter, S.R., Hill, J., Monfreda, C., Polasky, S., Rockström, J., Sheehan, J., Siebert, S., Tilman, D. and Zaks, D.P.M. (2011): "Solutions for a Cultivated Planet", *Nature* 478:337–342.

Foster, J.B. (2000): *Marx's Ecology: Materialism and Nature*. New York: Monthly Review Press.

Friedmann, H. (1993): "The Political Economy of Food: A Global Crisis", *New Left Review* 197:29–57.

Friedmann, H. and McMichael, P. (1989): "Agriculture and the State System: The Rise and Decline of National Agricultures, 1870 to the Present", *Sociologia Ruralis* 29(2):93–117.

Fröbel, F., Heinrichs, J. and Kreye, O. (1977): *Die neue internationale Arbeitsteilung: Strukturella Arbeitslogiskeit in den Industrieländern und die Industrialisierung der Entwicklungsländer*. Hamburg: Rowohlt.

*Gallagher Review of the Indirect Effects of Biofuels Production* (2008), Renewable Fuels Agency, www.unido.org/fileadmin/user_media/UNIDO_Header_Site/Subsites/Green_Industry_Asia_Conference__Maanila_/GC13/Gallagher_Report.pdf.

GAO [US Government Accountability Office] (2008): *Electronic Waste*, www.gao.gov/products/GAO-08-1044.

Garten Rothkopf (2009): *A Blue Print for Green Energy in the Americas*. Washington, DC: Inter-American Development Bank.

Georgescu-Roegen, N. (1971): *The Entropy Law and the Economic Process*. Cambridge: Harvard University Press.

Gibbs, H.K., Ruesch, A.S., Achard, F., Vlayton, M.K., Holmgren, P., Ramankutty, N. and Foley, J.A. (2010): "Tropical Forests were the Primary Sources of New Agricultural Land in the 1980s and 1990s", *Proceedings of the National Academy of Sciences* 107(38):16732–16737.

Giljum, S. and Eisenmenger, N. (2004): "North-South Trade and the Distribution of Goods and Burdens: A Biophysical Perspective", *Journal of Environment and Development* 13:73–100.

Global Footprint Network (2012a): "Introduction", *Footprint Science*, www.footprintnetwork.org/en/index.php/GFN/page/footprint_science_introduction/.

Global Footprint Network (2012b): *August 22 was Earth Overshoot Day*, www.footprintnetwork.org/en/index.php/GFN/page/earth_overshoot_day/.

GRAIN (2008): *Seized! The 2008 Land Grab for Food and Financial Security*, www.grain.org/article/entries/93-seized-the-2008-landgrab-for-food-and-financial-security.

Grilli, E.R. and Yang, M.C. (1988): "Primary Commodity Prices, Manufactured Goods Prices, and the Terms-of-trade of Developing Countries: What the Long Run Shows", *World Bank Economic Review* 2(1):1–47.

Grübler, A. (1998): *Technology and Global Change*. Cambridge: Cambridge University Press.

Gutierrez, A.P. and Ponti, L. (2009): "Bioeconomic Sustainability of Cellulosic Biofuel Production on Marginal Lands", *Bulletin of Science, Technology and Society* 29(3):213–225.

Haberl, H., Beringer, T., Bhattacharya, S.C., Erb, K.H. and Hoogwijk, M. (2010): "The Global Technical Potential of Bio-Energy in 2050 Considering Sustainability Constraints", *Current Opinion in Environmental Sustainability* 2:394–403.

Haberl, H., Erb, K.H., Krausmann, F., Gaube, V., Bondeau, A., Plutzar, C., Gingrich, S., Lucht, W. and Fischer-Kowalski, M. (2007): "Quantifying and Mapping the Human Appropriation of Net Primary Production in Earth's Terrestrial Ecosystems", *Proceedings of the National Academy of Sciences* 104(31):12942–12947.

Haberl, H., Wackernagel, M., Krausmann, F., Erb, K.H. and Monfreda, C. (2004): "Eco-logical Footprints and Human Appropriation of Net Primary Production: A Compari-son", *Land Use Policy* 21:279–288.

Hall, C.A.S., Balogh, S. and Murphy, J.R. (2009): "What is the Minimum EROI that a Sustainable Society Must Have?", *Sustainability* 2:25–47.

Hall, C.A.S., Dale, B.E. and Pimentel, D. (2011): "Seeking to Understand the Reasons for Different Energy Return on Investment (EROI) Estimates for Biofuels", *Sustainability* 3:263–282.

Hardin, G. (1968): "The Tragedy of the Commons", *Science* 13 December:1243–1248.

Hardin, G. (1998): "Extensions of the 'The Tragedy of the Commons'", *Science* 280:682–683.

Harrod, R.F. (1963): *The Life of John Maynard Keynes*. London: MacMillan.

Harvey, D.I., Kellard, N.M., Madsen, J.B. and Wohar, M.E. (2010): "The Prebisch–Singer Hypothesis: Four Centuries of Evidence", *The Review of Economics and Statistics* 92(2):367–377.

Hecht, S.B. (2005): "Soybeans, Development and Conservation on the Amazon Frontier", *Development and Change* 36(2):375–404.

Hoekstra, A.Y. and Chapagain, A.K. (2008): *Globalization of Water: Sharing the Plan-et's Freshwater Resources*. Malden: Blackwell.

Hoekstra, A.Y. and Hung, P.Q. (2005): "Globalisation of Water Resources: International Virtual Water Flows in Relation to Crop Trade", *Global Environmental Change* 15(1):45–56.

Hoekstra, A.Y. and Mekonnen, M.M. (2012): "The Water Footprint of Humanity", *Pro-ceedings of the National Academy of Sciences* 109(9):3232–3237.

Hollander, G. (2010): "Power is Sweet: Sugarcane in the Global Ethanol Assemblage", *Journal of Peasant Studies* 37(4): 699–721.

Holt-Giménez, E. and Shattuck, A. (2009): "The Agrofuels Transition: Restructuring Places and Spaces in the Global Food System", *Bulletin on Science, Technology and Society* 29(3):180–188.

Hoogwijk, M., Faaij, A., van den Broek, R., Berndes, G., Gielen, D. and Turkenburg, W. (2003): "Exploration of the Ranges of the Global Potential for Energy", *Biomass and Bioenergy* 25:119–133.

Hornborg, A. (2007a): "Footprints in the Cotton Fields: The Industrial Revolution as Time-Space Appropriation and Environmental Load Displacement", in Hornborg, A., McNeill, J.R. and Martínez-Alier, J., eds: *Rethinking Environmental History: World-System, History and Global Environmental Change*. Lanham, MD: Altamira Press.

Hornborg, A. (2007b): "Introduction: Environmental History as Political Ecology", in Horn-borg, A., McNeill, J.R. and Martínez-Alier, J.: *Rethinking Environmental History: World-System, History and Global Environmental Change*. Lanham, MD: Altamira Press.

Hornborg, A. and Crumley, C., eds (2007): *The World System and the Earth System: Global Socioenvironmental Change and Sustainability Since the Neolithic*. Walnut Creek, CA: Left Coast Press.

Hornborg, A., McNeill, J.R. and Martínez-Alier, J., eds (2007): *Rethinking Environmental History: World-System, History and Global Environmental Change*. Lanham, MD: Altamira Press.

IATP [Institute for Agriculture and Trade Policy] (2012*): Grain Reserves and the Food Price Crisis: Selected Writings from 2008–2012*, www.iatp.org/files/2012_07_13_ IATP_GrainReservesReader.pdf.

IEA (2009): *Key World Energy Statistics 2009*, Paris.

146   *References*

IEA (2011a): *Key World Energy Statistics 2011*, Paris.
IEA (2011b): *Technology Roadmap: Biofuels for Transport*, Paris.
IEA (2012): *World Energy Outlook 2012*, Paris.
IIED [International Institute for Environment and Development] (2011): *Are Land Deals Driving "Water Grabs"?* http://pubs.iied.org/17102IIED.html.
INPE [Instituto Nacional de Pesquisas Espaciais] (2009): *Taxa de desmatamento anual 1998–2009* [Annual deforestation rate 1998–2009] www.obt.inpe.br/prodes/prodes_1988_2009.htm.
INPE (2011): *Desmatatmento 2010–2011* [Deforestation 2010–2011], www.obt.inpe.br/prodes/r2011.htm.
IPCC (2007): *Fourth Assessment Report*, www.ipcc.ch/publications_and_data/ar4/syr/en/figure-spm-3.html.
IPCC (2011): *Special Report on Renewable Energy Sources and Climate Change Mitigation, Final Release*, http://srren.ipcc-wg3.de/report/IPCC_SRREN_Full_Report.
Jacobs, J. (1985): *Cities and the Wealth of Nations: Principles of Economic Life*. New York: Vintage Books.
Jorgenson, A.K. (2007): "Does Foreign Investment Harm the Air we Breathe and the Water we Drink?", *Oganization and Environment* 20(2)137–156.
Jorgenson, A.K. (2008): "Structural Integration and the Trees: An Analysis of Deforestation in Less-Developed Countries, 1990–2005", *The Sociological Quarterly* 49:503–527.
Jorgenson, A.K. (2009): "Foreign Direct Investment and the Environment, the Mitigating Influence of Institutional and Civil Society Factors, and Relationships between Industrial Pollution and Human Health", *Organization and Environment* 22:135–157.
Jorgenson, A.K. (2012): "The Sociology of Ecologically Unequal Exchange and Carbon Dioxide Emissions, 1960–2005", *Social Science Research* 41(2):242–252.
Jorgenson, A.K. and Kuykendall, K.A. (2008): "Globalization, Foreign Investment Dependence and Agriculture Production: Pesticide and Fertilizer Use in Less-Developed Countries, 1990–2000", *Social Forces* 87(1): 529–560.
Jorgenson, A.K., Austin, K. and Dick, C. (2009): "Ecologically Unequal Exchange and the Resource Consumption/Environmental Degradation Paradox: A Panel Study of Less-Developed Countries, 1970–2000", *International Journal of Comparative Sociology* 50:263–284.
Jorgenson, A.K., Dick, C. and Mahutga, M.C. (2007): "Foreign Investment Dependence and the Environment: An Ecostructural Approach", *Social Problems* 54(3):371–394.
Kaplinsky, R. (2006): "Revisiting the Revisited Terms-of-trade: Will China Make a Difference?", *World Development* 34(6):981–995.
Kaufman, F. (2010): "The Food Bubble: How Wall Street Starved Millions and Got Away With It", *Harper's Magazine*, July.
Kellard, N. and Wohar, M. (2006): "On the Prevalence of Trends in Primary Commodity Prices", *Journal of Development Economics* 79:146–167.
Keynes, J.M. (2007/1936): *The General Theory of Employment, Interest and Money*. New Delhi: Atlantic Publishers.
Kissinger, M. and Rees, W.E. (2009): "Footprints on the Prairies: Degradation and Sustainability of Canadian Agricultural Land in a Globalizing World", *Ecological Economics* (68):2309–2315.
Kissinger, M. and Rees, W.E. (2010): "Exporting Natural Capital: The Foreign Eco-Footprint on Costa Rica and Implications for Sustainability", *Environment, Development and Sustainability* (12):547–560.

Kitzes, J., Peller, A., Goldfinger, S. and Wackernagel, M. (2007): "Current Methods for Calculating National Ecological Footprint Accounts", *Science for Environment and Sustainable Society* 4(1):1–9.

Kjærgaard, T. (1994): *The Danish Revolution 1500–1800: An Ecohistorical Interpretation*, Cambridge: Cambridge University Press.

Klare, M. (2002): *Resource Wars: The New Landscape of Global Conflict*. New York: Holt.

Krausmann, F., Fischer-Kowalski, M., Schandl, H. and Eisenmengar, N. (2008): "The Global Sociometabolic Transition: Past and Present Metabolic Profiles and Their Future Trajectories", *Journal of Industrial Ecology* 12(56):637–656.

Krausmann, F., Gingrich, S., Eisenmenger, N., Erb, K.H., Haberl, H., Fischer-Kowalski, M. (2009): "Growth in Global Materials Use, GDP and Population During the 20th Century", *Ecological Economics* 68(10):2696–2705.

Krugman, P. (2009): "The Malthusian Insult", *New York Times*, 1 July, http://krugman.blogs.nytimes.com/2009/07/01/the-malthusian-insult/.

Krugman, P. and Obstfeld, M. (1994): *International Economics: Theory and Policy*. New York: HarperCollins.

Levy, D. and Peart, S. (2001): *The Secret History of the Dismal Science*, www.econlib.org/library/Columns/LevyPeartdismal.html.

Linnér, B.O. (1998): *The World Household: Georg Borgström and the Postwar Population-Resource Crisis*, Linköping University.

Lonergan, S.C. (1988): "Theory and Measurement of Unequal Exchange: A Comparison Between a Marxist Approach and an Energy Theory of Value", *Ecological Modelling* 41:127–145.

Lundqvist, J., Garron, J., Berndes, G., Berntell, A., Falkenmark, M., Karlberg, L. and Rockström, J. (2007): "Water Pressure and Increases in Food and Bioenergy Demand", *Scenarios on Eonomic Growth and Resource Demand*, background report to the Swedish Environmental Advisory Council Memorandum 2007:1, Stockholm.

MA [Millennium Assessment] (2005): *Millennium Ecosystem Assessment Synthesis Report*, www.millenniumassessment.org.

Mackey, L. (2011): "Legitimating Foreignization in Bolivia: Brazilian Agriculture and the Relations of Conflict and Consent in Santa Cruz, Bolivia", International Conference on Global Land Grabbing, Institute of Development Studies, University of Sussex.

Malthus, T.R. (2004/1798): *An Essay on the Principle of Population*. Oxford: Oxford University Press.

Mani, M. and Wheeler, D. (1998): "In Search of Pollution Havens? Dirty Industry in the World Economy 1960–1995", *The Journal of Environment Development* 7:215–247.

Martínez-Alier, J. (1990): *Ecological Economics: Energy, Environment and Society*, Oxford: Blackwell.

Martínez-Alier, J. (2002): *The Environmentalism of the Poor: A Study of Ecological Conflicts and Valuation*. Cheltenham: Edward Elgar Publishing.

Marx, K. (1990/1867): *Capital*, Volume 1. London: Penguin Classics.

Mathews, E., Amann, C., Bringezu, S., Fischer-Kowalski, M., Hüttler, W., Kleijn, R., Moriguchi, Y., Ottke, C., Eodenburg, E., Rogich, D., Schandl, H., Schütz, H., van den Voet, E. and Weisz, H. (2000): *The Weight of Nations: Material Outflows from Industrial Economies*, Washington, DC: World Resources Institute.

McMichael, P. (2009a): "A Food Regime Analysis of the 'World Food Crisis'", *Agriculture and Human Values* 26:281–295.

McMichael, P. (2009b): "A Food Regime Genealogy", *Journal of Peasant Studies* 36(1):139–169.

Mendonça, M.L. (2010): *Monopólio da terra no Brasil* [Land monopoly in Brazil], Rede Social de Justiça e Direitos Humanos, São Paulo, www.social.org.br/index. php?option=com_contentandview=articleandid=124:o-monopolio-da-terra-e-os-direitos-humanos-.

Mitchell, D. (2008): *A Note on Rising Food Prices*, Policy Research Working Paper 4682. Washington, DC: World Bank.

Moen, A.M. (2008): "Breaking Basel: The Elements of the Basel Convention and its Application to Toxic Ships", *Marine Policy* 32:1053–1062.

Monsanto (2009): Monsanto's Biofuel Story: Food and Fuel – It's not an "either/or" equation, www.monsanto.com/monsanto_today/for_the_record/biofuels.asp (accessed 24 December 2009, later deleted from Monsanto's website).

Moraes, M.A.F.D. de (2007): "O Mercado de trabalho da agroindústria canavieira: Desafios e oportunidades" [The sugarcane agro-industry labour market: Challenges and opportunities], *Economia Aplicada* 11(4):605–619.

Müller, C., Bondeau, A., Lotze-Campen, H., Cramer, W. and Lucht, W. (2006): "Comparative Impact of Climatic and Nonclimatic Factors on Global Terrestrial Carbon and Water Cycles", *Global Biochemical Cycles* 20:GB4015.

Muñoz Jaramillo, P.A. (2011): *Essays on International Trade and Environment: An Input-Output Analysis*, Institute of Environment Science and Technology, Autonomous University of Barcelona.

Murphy, D.J. and Hall, C.A.S. (2011): "Energy Return on Investment, Peak Oil, and the the End of Economic Growth", *Annals of the New York Academy of Sciences* 1219:52–72.

Myers, N., Mittermeier, R.A., Mittermeier, C.G., da Fonseca, G.A.B. and Kent, J. (2000): "Biodiversity hotspots for conservation priorities", *Nature* 403:853–858.

Nalepa, R.A. and Bauer, D.M. (2012): "Marginal Lands: The Role of Remote Sensing in Constructing Landscapes for Agrofuel Development", *Journal of Peasant Studies* 39(2):403–422.

*Nature* (2010): "Intensive Farming May Ease Climate Change", *Nature* 17 June.

Neves do Amaral, W.A., Marinho, J.P., Tarasantchi, R., Beber, A. and Giuliani, E. (2008): "Environmental Sustainability of Sugarcane Ethanol in Brazil", in Zuurbier, P. and van den Vooren, J., eds: *Sugarcane Ethanol: Contribution to Climate Change Mitigation and the Environment*, Wageningen: Wageningen Academic Publishers.

Newcombe, K., Kalma J.D. and Aston, A.R. (1978): "The Metabolism of a City: The Case of Hong Kong", *AMBIO* 7(1):3–15.

NGO Shipbreaking Platform (2007): *Comments on the EU Commission's Green Paper on Better Ship Dismantling*, www.shipbreakingplatform.org.

Novo, A., Jansen, K., Slingerland, M. and Giller, K. (2010): "Biofuel, Dairy Production and Beef in Brazil: Competing Claims on Land Use in São Paulo State", *Journal of Peasant Studies* 37 (4):769–792.

NR 31 [Norma Regulamentadora Rural 31] (2005): Segurança e saúde no trabalho de agricultura, pecuária silvicultura, exploração florestal e aqüicultura [Work safety and health in agriculture, cattle, forestry, logging and aquaculture], Ministério de trabalho e emprego, Brasília.

Oakland Institute (2011): *The Role of False Climate Change Solutions*, www.oaklandinstitute.org/land-deal-brief-role-false-climate-change-solutions.

Ocampo, J.A. and Parra, M.A. (2003): "The Terms-of-trade for Commodities in the Twentieth Century", *CEPAL Review* 79:7–35.

Odum, H.T. (1996): *Environmental Accounting: Energy and Environmental Decision Making*. New York: Wiley.

OECD (2011): *Towards Green Growth: Monitoring Progress – OECD Indicators*, www.oecd.org/dataoecd/37/33/48224574.pdf.

Olsson, L., Tambang, Y.G., Faran, T. and Jerneck, A. (2012): *Internationell handel med jordbruksmark: Ett modernt baggböleri* [International trade in agricultural lands], Lund University www.lucsus.lu.se/2012_LSLA_Rapport.pdf.

Open Letter (2010) to the Speaker of the House of Representatives and the Majority Leader of the Senate, www.usclimatenetwork.org/resource-database/ninety-scientists-to-pelosi-and-reid-on-addressing-biomass-carbon-accounting.

Ostrom, E. (1990): *Governing the Commons*. Cambridge: Cambridge University Press.

Oxfam (2011a): *Growing a Better Future: Food Justice in a Resource-constrained World*, www.oxfam.org/sites/www.oxfam.org/files/growing-a-better-future-010611-en.pdf.

Oxfam (2011b): *Land and Power: The Growing Scandal Surrounding the New Wave of Investments in Land*, Oxfam Briefing Paper 151, www.oxfam.org/sites/www.oxfam.org/files/bp151-land-power-rights-acquisitions-220911-summ-en.pdf.

Oxfam (2012): *The Hunger Grains*, Oxfam Briefing Paper 161, www.oxfam.org/sites/www.oxfam.org/files/bp161-the-hunger-grains-170912-en.pdf.

Pellow, D.N. (2007): *Resisting Global Toxics: Transnational Movements for Environmental Justice*. Cambridge, MA: MIT Press.

Peters, C.J., Wilkins, J.L. and Fick, G.W. (2007): "Testing a Complete-Diet Model for Estimating the Land Resource Requirements of Food Consumption and Agricultural Carrying Capacity: The New York State Example", *Renewable Agriculture and Food Systems* 22(2):145–153.

Peters, G.P. and Hertwich, E.G. (2006): "The Importance of Imports for Household Environmental Impacts", *Journal of Industrial Ecology* 10 (3):89–146.

Peters, G.P. and Hertwich, E.G. (2008): "$CO_2$ Embodied in International Trade with Implications for Global Climate Policy", *Environmental Science and Technology* 42 (5):1401–1407.

Peters, G.P., Minx, J.C., Weber, C.L. and Edenhofer, O. (2011): "Growth in Emission Transfers via International Trade from 1990 to 2008", *Proceedings of the National Academy of Sciences* 108(21):8903–8909.

Pietrafesa, J.P., Acelo, J.M. and Sauer, S. (2009): *Agroindústria canavieira no estado de Goiás: Ocupação de novos espaços em áreas de Cerrado* [Sugarcane agro-industry in Goiás: Opening up new space in the Cerrado], 33 Encontro anual da Associação Nacional de Pós-Graduação e Pesquisa em Ciências Sociais (ANPOCS), São Paulo.

Pietrafesa, J.P., Sauer, S. and dos Santos, A.E.A.F. (2010): *Expansão das lavouras de cana em Goiás: Ocupação de novos espaços em land areas de Cerrado e financiamento público* [Expansion of sugarcane cultivation in Goiás: Opening up new space in the Cerrado and public finance], VIII Congreso Latinoamericano de Sociologia Rural, Porto de Galinhas.

Pinstrup-Andersen, P., Pandya-Lorch, R. and Rosegrant, M.W. (1999): *World Food Prospects: Critical Issues for the Early Twenty-first Century*. Washington, DC: International Food Policy Research Institute.

Pires de Camargo, A.M.M., Caser, D.V., Pires de Camargo, F., Olivette, M.P. de A., Sachs, R.C.C. and Torquato, S.A. (2008): "Dinâmica e tendência de expansão da cana-de-açúcar sobre as demais atividades agropecuárias, estado de São Paulo, 2001–2006" [Dynamics and trends of sugarcane expansion compared to other agriculture and livestock in São Paulo 2001–2006], *Informações Econômicas, SP* 38(3):47–66.

Plancherel, A.A., Queiroz, A.S., da Silva, B.S. and da Santos, C. (undated): *Perfil do cana-vieiro e relações de trabalho na atual agroindústria de Alagoas* [Sugarcane profile and labour relations in Alagoas agro-industry], www.estudosdotrabalho.org/anais-vii-7-seminario-trabalho-ret-2010/Alice_Plancherel_Allan_Queiroz_Barbara_Silva_Charles_Santos_perfil_canavieiro_e_relacoes_de_trabalho_agroindustria_acucareira_alagoas.pdf.

Polanyi, K. (2002/1944): *The Great Transformation: The Political and Economic Origins of Our Time*. Boston: Beacon.

Pomeranz, K. (2000): *The Great Divergence: Europe, China and The Making of the Modern World Economy*. Princeton: Princeton University Press.

Prebisch, R. (1950): *The Economic Development of Latin America and its Principal Problems*. New York: United Nations.

Prebisch, R. (1984): "Five Stages in My Thinking on Development", in Meier, G.M. and Seers, D., eds: *Pioneers in Development*. Cambridge: Oxford University Press.

Projeto de Lei (2008), Dispõe sobre a regulamentação da automação/mencanização na atividade canavieira [Regulation of the automation/mechanization of sugarcane cultivation], Assembléia legislativa, Estado de Goiás, elaborated by Isaura Lemos, Partido Democrático Trabalhista [Democratic Labour Party].

Protocolo de cooperação (2007), www.ambiente.sp.gov.br/etanolverde/files/2011/10/protocoloAgroindustriais.pdf.

RAI [Responsible Agro-Investment] (2012): *Principles for Responsible Agricultural Investment (RAI) that Respects Rights, Livelihoods and Resources*, www.responsibleagroinvestment.org/rai/node/256.

Ravindranath, N.H., Manuvie, R., Fargione, J., Canadell, J.G., Berndes, G., Woods, J., Watson, H. and Sathaye, J. (2009): "Greenhouse Gas Implications of Land Use and Land Conversion to Biofuel Crops", in Howarth, R.W. and Bringezu, S., eds: *Proceedings of the Scientific Committee on Problems of the Environment, International Biofuels Project Rapid Assessment*, Cornell University.

Rede Social de Justiça e Direitos Humanos (2008): *Direitos Humanos e a Indústria da Cana* [Regulation of the automation/mechanization of sugarcane cultivation], São Paulo.

REN21 [Renewable Energy Policy Network for the 21st Century] (2011): *Renewables 2011: Global Status Report*, Milan.

Repórter Brasil (2010): *Brazil of Biofuels: Sugarcane 2009*, São Paulo, www.reporterbrasil.org.br/documentos/brazil_of_biofuels_v6.pdf.

Repórter Brasil (2011): *BNDES and Its Environmental Policy*, www.reporterbrasil.org.br/documentos/BNDES_English.pdf.

Ricardo, R. (2006/1817): *Principles of Political Economy and Taxation*. New York: Cosimo Classics.

Richardson, K., Will, S., Schellnhuber, H.J., Alcamo, J., Barker, T., Kammen, D.M., Leemans, R., Liverman, D., Munasinghe, M., Osman-Elasha, B., Stern, N. and Wæver, O. (2009): *Climate Change: Global Risks, Challenges and Decisions – Synthesis Report*, http://climatecongress.ku.dk/pdf/synthesisreport.

Roll, E. (1961): *A History of Economic Thought*. London: Faber.

Röpke, I. (2004): "The Early History of Modern Ecological Economics", *Ecological Economics* 50:293–314.

Rosenfeld, P.E. and Feng, L.G.H. (2011): *Risks of Hazardous Wastes*. Burlington, MA: Elsevier.

Royal Swedish Academy of Sciences (2009): *The Prize in Economic Sciences 2009*, www.nobelprize.org/nobel_prizes/economics/laureates/2009/popular-economicsciences2009.pdf.

RSB (2010): *RSB Principles and Criteria for Sustainable Biofuel Production*, version 2.0 http://rsb.epfl.ch/page-67254-en.html.

RSB (2012): *RSB's First Phase 2006–2009*, http://rsb.epfl.ch/page-51764-en.html.

Rulli, M.C., Saviori, A. and D'Odorico, P. (2013): "Global Land and Water Grabbing", *Proceedings of the National Academy of Sciences*, www.pnas.org/content/early/2013/01/02/1213163110.

Sarkar, P. and Singer, H.W. (1991): "Manufactured Exports of Developing Countries and Their Terms-of-trade Since 1965", *World Development* 19(4):333–340.

Sassen, S. (2006): *Territory Authority Rights: From Medieval to Global Assemblages.* Princeton: Princeton University Press.

Sawyer, D. (2008): "Climate Change, Biofuels and Eco-Social Impacts in the Brazilian Amazon and Cerrado", *Philosophical Transactions of the Royal Society B* (363):1747–1752.

Sawyer, D. (2009): "Fluxos de carbono na Amazônia e no Cerrado: Um olhar socioecossistêmico" [The flow of carbon in the Amazon and the Cerrado: A socio-ecosystemic view], *Sociedade e Estado*, 24(1):149–171.

Schandl, H. and Krausmann, F (2007): "The Local Base of the Historical Agrarian-Industrial Transition and the Interaction Between Scales", in Fischer-Kowalski, M. and Haberl, H., eds: *Socioecological Transitions and Global Change.* Cheltenham: Edward Elgar.

Searchinger, T., Heimlich, R., Houghton, R.A., Dong, F., Elobeid, A., Fabiosa, J., Tokgoz, S., Hayes, D. and Yu, T.-H. (2008): "Use of US Croplands for Biofuels Increases Greenhouse Gases Through Emissions from Land-Use Change", *Science* 319:1238–1240.

Seto, K.C., Güneralp, B. and Hutyra, L.R. (2012): "Global Forecasts of Urban Expansion to 2030 and Direct Impacts on Biodiversity and Carbon Pools", *Proceedings of the National Academy of Sciences*, early edition, www.pnas.org/content/early/2012/09/11/1211658109.full.pdf+html.

Shandra, J.M., Leckband, C., McKinney, L. and London, B. (2009): "Ecologically Unequal Exchange: World Polity, and Biodiversity Loss – A Cross-National Analysis of Threatened Mammals", *International Journal of Comparative Sociology* 50(3–4):285–310.

Sieferle, R.P. (2001): *The Subterranean Forest: Energy Systems and the Industrial Revolution.* Cambridge: White Horse Press.

Silva, M.A. de M. (2008): *Trabalhadores rurais: A negação dos direitos*, São Paulo: Rede Social de Justiça e Direitos Humanos.

Silva, M.A. de M. (2010): "A degradação social do trabalho e da natureza no contexto da monocultura canavieira paulista" [The social degradation of work and nature in sugarcane monoculture in São Paulo], *Sociologias* 12(24):196–240.

Silva, M.A. de M. and Ribeiro, J.D. (2010): *Violação dos direitos e formas de resistência nos canaviais paulistas* [Violations of rights and forms of resistance in the São Paulo sugarcane fields], VIII Congresso Latinomericano de Sociologia Rural, Porto de Galinhas, www.alasru.org/wp-content/uploads/2011/09/GT21-MARIA-APARECIDA-DE-MORAES-SILVA.pdf.

Singer, H.W. (1950): "The Distribution of Gains between Investing and Borrowing Countries", *American Economic Review* 40(2):473–485.

Singer, H.W. (1984): "The Terms-of-trade Controversy and the Evolution of Soft Financing: Early Years in the UN", in Meier, G.M. and Seers, D., eds: *Pioneers in Development.* Oxford: Oxford University Press.

Skidelsky, R. (2000): *John Maynard Keynes: Fighting for Britain 1937–1946.* London: Penguin.

Smeets, E., Junginger, M., Faaij, A., Walter, A. and Dolzan, P. (2006): *Sustainability of Brazilian Bio-Ethanol,* Unicamp/Universiteit Utrecht.

Smeets, E.M.W., Faaij, A.P.C., Lewandowski, I.M. and Turkenburg, W.C. (2007): "A Bottom-Up Assessment and Review of Global Bio-Energy Potentials to 2050", *Progress in Energy and Combustion Sciences* 33:56–106.

Smil, V (2005): "21st Century Energy: Some Sobering Thoughts", *OECD Observer* 258/259:22–23.

Sparovek, G., Barretto, A., Klug, I., Papp, L. and Lino, J. (2010a): *A idéia de substituir o Código Florestal* [The proposed replacement of the forest code], Universidade de São Paulo, Piracicaba.

Sparovek, G., Berndes, G., Klug, I.L.F. and Barretto, A.G.O.P. (2010): "Brazilian Agriculture and Environmental Legislation: Status and Future Challenges", *Environmental Science and Technology* 44(6):6046–6053.

Srinivasan, U.T., Carey, S.P., Hallstein, E., Higgins, P.A.T., Kerr, A.C., Koteen, L.E., Smith, A.B., Watson, R., Harte, J. and Norgaards, R.B. (2008): "The Debt of Nations and the Distribution of Ecological Impacts from Human Activities", *Proceedings of the National Academy of Sciences* 105(5):1768–1773.

Summers, L. (1991): "Memo on Dirty Industries", www.globalpolicy.org/component/content/article/212/45462.html.

Swedish EPA (2008): *Konsumtionens klimatpåverkan* [Consumption and climate change], Rapport 5903, Stockholm.

Tilman, D., Socolow, R., Foley, J.A., Hill, J., Larson, E., Lynd, L., Pacala, S., Reilly, J., Searchinger, T., Sommerville, C. and Williams, R. (2009): "Beneficial Biofuels – The Food, Energy and Environment Trilemma", *Science* 325:270–271.

UN (2009): *World Population Prospects: The 2008 Revision,* www.un.org/esa/population/publications/wpp. 2008/wpp. 2008_text_tables.pdf.

UN (2011): *World Population Prospects: The 2010 Revision,* http://esa.un.org/wpp/Documentation/pdf/WPP2010_Highlights.pdf.

UNCTAD (2008): *Making Certification Work for Sustainable Development: The Case of Biofuels,* New York.

UNCTAD (2011): *Commodities At a Glance,* March 2011, New York.

UNDP [United Nations Development Programme] (2003): *Making Global Trade Work for People.* London: Earthscan.

UNEP (2009): *Towards Sustainable Production and Use of Resources: Assessing Biofuels,* Nairobi.

UNFCCC (2012): *Outcome of the work of the Ad Hoc Working Group on Further Commitments for Annex I Parties under the Kyoto Protocol,* http://unfccc.int/resource/docs/2012/cmp8/eng/l09.pdf.

UNICA (2009): *Etanol e bioelectricidade: A cana-de-açúcar no futuro da matriz energética,* São Paulo.

UNICA (2010): Comments by UNICA to the European Commission's Consultation on Indirect Land Use Change Impacts of Biofuels, 29 October 2010, http://english.unica.com.br/download.asp?mmdCode={1B7F9877-BDD0–4B66–8959–1E4BB6012AE8}.

UNICA (2011a): *Sugarcane Industry in Brazil* http://english.unica.com.br/download.asp?mmdCode=BF2F6A2B-F95F-4CC6–84E1–23C834D981BE.

UNICA (2011b): *Sustainability Report 2010,* http://english.unica.com.br/download.asp?mmdCode=30C5CC87–4093–4826–95D6–5ECF8D7E224A.

USDA [United States Department of Agriculture] (2009): *World Agricultural Production*, http://usda.mannlib.cornell.edu/MannUsda/viewDocumentInfo.do?documentID=1860.

Via Campesina, FIAN International, Focus on the Global South and Rede Social (2010): *Why We Oppose the Principles for Responsible Agricultural Investment*, www.viacampesina.org/en/images/stories/pdf/whyweopposerai.pdf.

Vitousek, P.M., Ehrlich, P.R., Ehrlich, A.H. and Matson, P.A (1986): "Human Appropriation of the Products of the Photosynthesis", *BioScience* 36(6):368–373.

von Braun, J. (2008): *Biofuels, International Food Prices, and the Poor*, Washington, DC: International Food Policy Research Institute.

Wackernagel, M. and Rees, W. (1996): *Our Ecological Footprint: Reducing Human Impact on the Earth*. Philadelphia: New Society Publishers.

Warren, B. (1980): *Imperialism: Pioneer of Capitalism*. London: New Left Books.

Warren-Rhodes, K. and Koenig, A (2001): "Ecosystem Appropriation by Hong Kong and its Implications for Sustainable Development", *Ecological Economics* 39:347–359.

WBGU [Wissenschaftliger Beirat der Bundesregiering Globale Umweltveränderungen] (2009): *Welt im Wandel: Zukunfstfähige Bioenergie und nachhaltige Landnutzung*, Berlin.

WEF (2011): *Global Risks 2011*. Sixth Edition, Geneva.

Weisz, H. (2007); "Combining Social Metabolism and Input-Output Analyses", in Hornborg, A., McNeill, J.R. and Martínez-Alier, J., eds: *Rethinking Environmental History: World-System History and Global Environmental Change*. Lanham, MD: Altamira Press.

Wilkinson, J. and Herrera, S. (2010): "Biofuels in Brazil: Debates and Impacts", *Journal of Peasant Studies* 37(4):749–768.

Wilkinson, R.G. (1973): *Poverty and Progress: An Ecological Model of Economic Development*. London: Methuen.

Wily, L.A. (2011): *The Tragedy of Public Lands: The Fate of the Commons under Global Commercial Pressure*, International Land Coalition, www.landcoalition.org/sites/default/files/publication/901/WILY_Commons_web_11.03.11.pdf.

Wirsenius, S. (2003): "Efficiencies and Biomass Appropriation of Food Commodities on Global and Regional Levels", *Agricultural Systems* 77:219–255.

Wirsenius, S., Azar, C. and Berndes, G. (2010): "How Much Land Is Needed for Global Food Production Under Scenarios of Dietary Changes and Livestock Productivity Increases in 2030", *Agricultural Systems* 103:621–638.

World Bank (2007): *Agriculture for Development*, World Development Report 2008, Washington, DC.

World Bank (2008): *International Trade and Climate Change: Economic, Legal, and Institutional Perspectives*, Washington, DC.

World Bank (2009): *Awakening Africa's Sleeping Giant: Prospects for Commercial Agriculture in the Guinea Savannah Zone and Beyond*, Washington, DC.

World Bank (2010): *Ship Breaking and Recycling Industry in Bangladesh and Pakistan*, Report 58275-SAS.

World Bank (2011): *Rising Global Interest in Farmland: Can it Yield Sustainable and Equitable Benefits?*, Washington, DC.

Worster, D. (1994): *Nature's Economy: A History of Ecological Ideas*. Cambridge: Cambridge University Press.

WRI [World Resources Institute] (2005): *World Greenhouse Gas Emissions in 2005*, www.wri.org/image/view/11147/_original.

Wrigley, E.A. (1988): *Continuity, Chance and Change: The Character of the Industrial Revolution in England*. Cambridge: Cambridge University Press.

WTO (2009, 2011): *International Trade Statistics 2009, 2011,* www.wto.org/english/res_e/statis_e/its_e.htm.

Wunder, S. (2008): "How Do We Deal with Leakage?", Angelsen, A., ed: *Moving Ahead with REDD: Issues, Options and Implications,* CIFOR, www.cifor.org/publications/pdf_files/Books/BAngelsen0801.pdf.

WWF (2008): *The Living Planet Report 2008,* http://awsassets.panda.org/downloads/living_planet_report_2008.pdf.

WWF Brasil (2011): *Código Florestal: Entenda o que está em jogo com a reforma da nossa legislação ambiental* [The forest code: Understand the stakes in the reform of our environmental legislation], www.wwf.org.br/informacoes/blibliioteca/?27443/Codigo-Florestal-Entenda-o-que-esta-em-jogo-com-a-reforma-de-nossa-legislacao-ambiental.

Zania, G.P. (2005): "Testing for Trends in the Terms-of-trade between Primary Commodities and Manufactures Goods", *Journal of Development Economics* 78:49–59.

Zoneamento agroecológico da cana-de-açucar (2010), www.cnps.embrapa.br/zoneamento_cana_de_acucar/.

# Index

Page numbers in *italics* denote tables, those in **bold** denote figures.

Cronon, William 15–16
curse of resources 104–5, *105*

Daewoo 118
Daly, Herman 84
Deere 120
deforestation: Brazil 53, 124; global 2,
    132–4, *133*; scenarios 124
Dell computers 111
Denmark 78; ecological relief 14; indirect
    flows 100
dismal science 7
Dominican Republic 111
Dow 58
Dreyfus 58
DTA 96; Norway 99; Sweden 99
Dupont 111, 120

ECLA 55
ecological economics 83–6, *83*
ecological exchange, measures 86–90,
    92–105
ecological footprints 86–8, 92–3, **93**; Hong
    Kong 16
ecological relief 14
ecological windfalls 12, 14
ecologically unequal exchange: defined 92;
    compared and interpreted 96–105
economy: organic 12; mineral 13
Ecuador 100
Egypt: EUE 104; food riots 116; food
    reserves 117; water grab 121
Eisenhower, Dwight D. 132
electronic waste exports 113–14
embodied: labour 12; land 12, 71–2, *90*
Emmanuel, Arrighi 71, 78–9, 104, 136
energy supply, global 23, **23**
Engels, Friedrich 9, 136
environmental economics 83–5, *83*
environmental load displacements 109–21
EROI 122–3
Ethiopia: food reserves 117; land grab 118
EU: agrofuels displace food 22; indirect
    land use change 60; raw materials
    diplomacy 129–30; RED 23–4, 60,
    64–5; WTO 127–8
exports: embodied land and labour 12,
    71–2, *90*; e-waste 113–14; pesticides
    110–1; waste 110–11
extractive economy 79–80

FAO 21–2, 25–6, 38, 55, 110–11, 134–5
FDIs 114, *115*
fictitious commodities 135

financialization: food price increase 20–1;
    land 135–6
food: crop productivity increase 132;
    drivers of price rise 19–22; future 76–7;
    global demand 25; prices 19–22, **20**;
    regimes 125, *126*; reserves 117
fossil fuel scenarios 123–5, *124–5*
fungibility of land 22–3
France: "slaves" 13; *SS France* 112–13
Franklin, Benjamin 7, 137
Friedmann, Harriet 125–6
fungibility of land 22–3

*Gallagher Review of the Indirect Effects of
    Biofuels* 24, 32
García, Alan 136
GATT 126–7
geographic rift 81
geopolitics and agrofuels 23–4, 31, 62, 67,
    116, 124
Georgescu-Roegen, Nicholas 84
Germany 102, 117; indirect flows 100
global overshoot day 88
Goldman Sachs 20
GRAIN 115–16
Great Britain 102; exchange of embodied
    labour and land 12–14; imports from
    India 15; water grab
greenhouse gas emissions 128
guano 9
Guinea-Bissau 111

Haig, Alexander 18
Haiti 111; food riots 116
Hardin, Garrett 42–3
Honduras 111; food riots 116
Hong Kong, ecological footprint 16
Hornborg, Alf 12, 81
human appropriation of net primary
    production 89, 94–6, *95*

IEA: acceptable agrofuel feedstocks 65;
    world energy outlook to 2020 123
IFAD 135
India 58; export of grain 1875–1900 15;
    export plans 117; EUE 101; famine 18;
    land grab 119; ship breaking 113;
    supreme court ruling 113, 136; water
    grab 121
indirect flows of materials and resources
    99–100
Indonesia: agrofuels 21, 31, 64;
    deforestation 124; food reserves 117;
    food riots 116; waste dump 111